The Trivia Lovers'
Guide To

CRICKET

The Trivia Lovers'
Guide To

CRICKET

First published in 2007
Reprinted in 2009

The views expressed in this book are those of the author but they are
general views only and readers are urged to consult a relevant and
qualified specialist for individual advice in particular situations.

Packaged by Susanna Geoghegan HP2 6HG
Cover and design by Peter Wilkinson
Typeset by David Onyett, Publishing & Production Services, Cheltenham
Printed in China

Introduction

'Cricket began when first a man-monkey, instead of catching a cocoa-nut thrown him playfully by a fellow-anthropoid, hit it away from him with a stick which he chanced to be holding in his hand.'

So wrote one Horace Hutchinson in a book published in 1903, but the game as we know it started in the south-east of England and centred around the counties of Kent, Surrey and Sussex. Cricket seems initially to have been played mainly by boys, and matches were probably largely chaotic in nature. However it started, it's clear that cricket soon increased in popularity in the south-east, although it took quite a while to reach other parts of the country. Landed gentry were largely responsible for the game's development; as they took to it they introduced it to some of the public schools, and it naturally graduated from there to Oxford and Cambridge Universities.

Cricket has since spread all over the world – initially through the Commonwealth, but now even more widely. Coverage ranges from newspapers and magazines, through radio and television to the Internet, and the stories, facts and figures surrounding this great game are too many to count. The myth and legend surrounding the great figures of the game, from W. G. Grace through Boycott, Botham and Lillee to Freddie Flintoff, is almost as entertaining as watching them play. And then there's the small matter of knowing your ODIs from your MCC!

We've gathered between these covers a selection of fascinating facts, figures and trivia with the intention of entertaining the reader in those inevitable breaks when rain stops play. So whether you're a die-hard cricket-watcher on the boundary, or prefer your sport to come to your living room through the small screen, keep it handy as you savour cricket in its many forms.

CRICKET

Cricket Timeline

A few notable, and perhaps not so notable, events in the history of the game.

1598   During a court case at Guildford, Surrey, a witness states that he and his friends had played 'creckett' on a disputed piece of land many years earlier (probably around 1550).

1613   A person is hit by someone using a 'cricket staff' in a hamlet near Guildford.

1622   A group of youths is accused of playing cricket in the churchyard of a village near Chichester in Sussex.

1624   A coroner's jury at West Hoathly, also in Sussex, is told of a man who had accidentally killed another with a small staff called a 'cricket batt'.

1700   Cricket matches are organised on Clapham Common (now in London) with the participants each betting £10 on the result.

1709   The first game between two county sides takes place – Kent versus Surrey, at Dartford. Sadly, the result has not survived.

1744   The Laws of Cricket are produced, although there were certainly earlier laws that have since been lost.

1744   The Sackville family of Sevenoaks issues a very special challenge: Kent would play the rest of England. Billed as 'The Greatest Cricket Match Ever Known' the result would be a victory for Kent by one wicket.

1751   A team representing New York plays the London Cricket Club, in New York.

Mid 1760s   Hambledon Cricket Club is founded in Hampshire.

1769   The first recorded century is scored by John Minishull for the Duke of Dorset's XI.

1787   Thomas Lord founds Marylebone Cricket Club (MCC) at Dorset Fields, Marylebone.

1794   Charterhouse play Westminster in the first recorded game between public schools.

1796   The Headmaster of Eton College flogs the Eton team for playing a match against his wishes. Presumably, he is a football fan.

1806   Gentlemen meet Players for the first time – at Lord's.

CRICKET

1811 A 'Grand Female Cricket Match' between Surrey and Hampshire is played over three days in September, at Robert Thornton Esq's Park near The Plough at Clapham. There is a prize of 500 Guineas (£525) and admission is One Shilling (5p).

1814 Having already moved once, MCC moves home again because too many people are turning up to watch matches, and the members are unhappy about all the rowdiness. The new ground comes to be known as Lord's.

1817 Perhaps the first case of match fixing takes place, when England play Nottingham. One William Lambert of Surrey is banned from Lord's for his part in the affair.

1825 Sussex play Kent, in a match that is widely recognised as being the one from which the official County Championship originated.

1859 The first England team goes overseas – to North America!

1864 Over-arm bowling becomes legal.

1876 W. G. Grace becomes the first player to score more than 300 runs in a first-class innings, when he makes 344, playing for MCC at Canterbury.

1877   The first recognised Test match is played between Australia and England, in Melbourne. The Aussies win it. What a surprise.

1880   The Oval stages its first Test match when England play Australia.

1884   Lord's stages its first Test. Naturally, Australia are again the opponents.

1890   The County Championship is formalised. Gloucestershire, Kent, Lancashire, Middlesex, Nottinghamshire, Surrey, Sussex and Yorkshire take part. Surrey win nine matches out of 14, and are declared champions.

1900   The six-ball over is introduced in England.

1905   The Australian Board of Control is established.

1909   The ICC is founded. At the time, the letters stand for Imperial Cricket Conference.

1928   The first Test match against the West Indies is played at Lord's.

1929   In Bridgetown, Barbados, the Kensington Oval stages its first Test – against England.

CRICKET

1932 India play their first Test match at Lord's.

1932–33 The 'bodyline series' takes place in Australia.

1947 The first ever first-class match is played in the newly created country of Pakistan.

1952 Pakistan join the International Cricket Council (ICC).

1958 Surrey win the County Championship for the seventh consecutive season.

1962 The last Gentlemen versus Players match takes place at Scarborough on 8th September. The Players win by seven wickets.

1968 South Africa refuse to accept Basil D'Oliviera as a member of the England touring side, because of the country's race laws. Cancellation of the tour leads to the sporting isolation of South Africa for many years.

1969 The Sunday League starts.

1977 Businessman Kerry Packer signs 51 Test players, not all of them has-beens, to create an 'outlaw' organisation, World Series cricket. It doesn't last.

1980   A new edition of the Laws of Cricket is published.

1992   Durham join the County Championship. They are the first new county to join for many decades.

1993   All County Championship matches are now to be played over four days, rather than three.

1997   The England and Wales Cricket Board is established.

2000   The County Championship is split into two divisions.

2005   England win the Ashes for the first time since 1987, and 25,000 people flock to Trafalgar Square to celebrate.

2006   England lose the Ashes again – whitewashed in Australia. Nobody goes anywhere near Trafalgar Square.

2007   England fail to qualify for the World Cup semi-finals, and coach Duncan Fletcher resigns. Bob Woolmer, formerly of Kent and England, and coach to the Pakistan side, dies on 18 March in his hotel room in Jamaica.

CRICKET

Woolley Bully

Kent and England batsman Frank Woolley, whose career ran more or less parallel with that of the great Jack Hobbs, played in 978 first-class matches and scored 58,969 runs at an average of 40.77.

Cricketing Wit and Wisdom I

'There's sarcastic applause from all around the ground – from those who are still awake.'
Ian Botham, commenting upon the scoring of a single, after a large number of dot balls, by England against Bangladesh during a Super Eight World Cup match in 2007

'Don't bother shutting it, son. You won't be there long enough.'
Fred Trueman to an incoming Australian batsman, as he opened the gate at Lord's

'The aim of English cricket is, in fact, mainly to beat Australia.'
Jim Laker

'A cricket tour in Australia would be the most delightful period in one's life, if one was deaf'.
Harold Larwood

'I suppose that Jeeves's bowling must have impressed me, for I remember him in 1916, and when I was in New York and starting the Jeeves and Bertie saga.'
P. G. Wodehouse, vaguely explaining that he named Bertie Wooster's butler after Warwickshire cricketer Percy Jeeves

Skirting the Issue

Long before women became accepted as real cricketers, they did feature in the occasional match. In September 1907, Nottinghamshire Ladies played Notts Crimea and Indian Mutiny Veterans, before 1,500 spectators. The proceeds of the event were to go towards a holiday home in Skegness for children of the Nottingham poor. The ladies inevitably wore long skirts, which must have made playing very difficult. They did very well however, making a total of 106. The game ended as a draw, with the veterans on 82–8.

Hall or Nothing

South African medium-pacer Andrew Hall was due to play for Kent once more during the 2007 County Championship campaign, so Kentish supporters were hoping he would be in fine form. Accordingly, they didn't know whether to laugh or cry when he took a career best 5 for 18 to humiliate England in the World Cup a few weeks earlier.

CRICKET

Cricketing Brothers

The legendary W. G. **Grace** had two brothers – E. M. and G .F. Grace. All three played in the same England v Australia match at the Oval in 1880.

Dave and Ned **Gregory** were brothers who both played for Australia in the first recognised Test match versus England, in Melbourne during 1877. Several other members of the Gregory family were cricketers, including Ned's son Syd, who made 58 Test appearances for Australia between 1890 and 1912.

Worcestershire had five brothers called **Foster** playing regularly in the 1908 County Championship season.

Henry William (Harry) **Lee**, who was born in 1890 and died in 1981, made 401 appearances for Middlesex. He had two brothers – F. S. Lee and J. W. Lee, both of whom played for Middlesex and Somerset.

John **Langridge**, who lived from 1910 until 1999, played for Sussex from 1928 until 1955. He was perhaps the finest batsman never to play in a Test match. He scored more than 34,000 runs and made 76 centuries for his county, and was also a fine slip fielder. He became an umpire upon his retirement. Meanwhile his older brother, James, was an all-rounder with Sussex for 30 years from 1924. James played in eight Tests and altogether made 31,716 runs, with 42 centuries. He also took 1,530 first-class wickets. James did not live anywhere near as long as his brother: he died aged 60 in 1966. His son Richard played for Sussex in the 1960s.

(Syed) Wazir **Ali** played in seven Tests for India between 1932 and 1936. He died aged 46, following an operation for appendicitis. His brother, (Syed) Nazir Ali, played for Sussex and made two Test match appearances for India.

There have been four Pakistani Test-playing **Mohammad** brothers. The eldest, Wazir, was born in 1929 and he featured in 20 Test matches for Pakistan between 1952 and 1959. Then came Hanif. He was born in 1934 and he went on to play in 55 Tests between 1952 and 1970. Mushtaq was born in 1943. He played in his first Test match in 1959, at the tender age of 15. He went on to play in 56 more Tests, and to captain the side on 19 occasions. An all-rounder, Mushtaq was an excellent batsman and a very good leg-spinner. He was also one of the very best reverse sweepers, and he played for Northamptonshire between 1966 and 1977. Finally, Sadiq was born in 1945. He featured in 41 Tests between 1969 and 1980. Sadiq was the only left-handed batsmen amongst the brothers.

Four Sri Lankan brothers also played first-class cricket.

CRICKET

Arjuna **Ranatunga**, born in Colombo in 1963, played in 93 Test matches and a total of 269 ODIs. A left-handed batsman who led Sri Lanka when they won the World Cup in 1996, he also featured in Sri Lanka's first Test match when he was only 18 years old. Arjuna's brothers were Sanjeeva, who played in nine Tests and 13 ODIs, Dammika – two Tests and four ODIs – and Nishantha, who played in just two ODIs.

The **Chappell** brothers – Ian and Greg – are probably the most famous of Australia's cricketing siblings. Ian, born in 1943, played in 75 Tests between 1964 and 1980, and had a batting average of 42.42. He often batted in partnership with brother Greg (born 1948) who made 87 Test match appearances between 1970 and 1984. Greg's Test batting average was an excellent 53.86. A third brother, Trevor, born 1952, played in just three Tests and 20 ODIs, while their grandfather, Vic Richardson, was an all-round sportsman who played Test cricket for Australia between 1924 and 1936.

Australia has also produced the **Lee** brothers – Brett and Shane. Brett Lee is a very fast bowler, one delivery having been recorded at 99.9 mph. Brother Shane was an all-rounder who played in England for Somerset and Worcestershire. Unfortunately, he was forced to retire at the age of 29, due to knee problems.

Won't Seymour

Seymour Clark was a wicketkeeper for Somerset. His first-class career was not a long one – it lasted just five matches – but in nine innings he made not a single run. Still, he was not out on two occasions.

Talking Cricket I

ASHES

When, in 1882, Australia beat England in England for the first time, it seemed that civiliszation, as every right-thinking cricket lover knew it, had come to an end. Someone decided to cremate one of the bails and place the ashes in an urn, to be offered to the Aussies as a trophy. The urn containing the Ashes in fact remains at Lord's, but it is normally in the theoretical possession of the Australians.

BALL TAMPERING

Ball tampering is deemed to have occurred when a member of the fielding side has deliberately scratched, roughened, or otherwise interfered with the condition of the ball, in order to gain an advantage. England captain Mike Atherton was found guilty of the offence in 1994, and more recently Pakistan were accused by umpire Darrell Hair – with most unfortunate consequences. Over the years, cricketers of all nations have in fact indulged in a bit of ball tampering.

CRICKET

BEAMER
A beamer is a ball aimed by the bowler straight at the batsman's head. It's usually accidental. Usually.

BODYLINE BOWLING
The English naturally never cheat at anything – especially cricket. Ask any Australian, and remind him (if he needs reminding) of the 'bodyline series' of 1932–33. During England's Ashes tour that winter, English fast bowler Harold Larwood perfected the art of bowling directly at the batsman, while packing the leg-side field. This resulted in a large number of leg-side catches, as well as quite a few injured batsmen. The Aussies were not amused, and the tactic was later banned by the authorities.

BOUNCER
A bouncer is a fast ball which pitches short and rises sharply. It is used to intimidate the batsman and also to encourage him to lash out and get himself caught near the boundary. In County and Test match cricket the delivery is not generally illegal, unless it is bowled frequently. Bouncers are frequently called as 'Wides' by umpires in one-day cricket.

BYES AND LEG BYES
Runs known as byes may be taken when the ball passes the batsman without touching his bat or his body. Wicketkeepers usually get the blame for byes, although

wild bowling is often the cause. Leg byes may be taken when the ball passes the bat but strikes any part of the batsman's body other than his hands.

Viv at Full Speed

The unstoppable Vivian Richards created the record for the fastest century in Test Cricket when he reached a hundred in an amazing 56 balls against England at St Johns in 1985–86.

For the Record: Test Matches I

The 1,000th Test match century was scored by Australia's Ian Chappell in 1968. Fourteen years later Ian's brother, Greg, scored the 1,500th Test century.

Australia beat England in the first recognised Test match by 45 runs. That was in 1877. When the Centenary Test was played a hundred years later, Australia again won by 45 runs. Both matches were played in Melbourne.

The Surrey off-spinner Jim Laker took 9–37 in first innings in the Fourth Test against Australia, at Old Trafford in 1956. He then took 10–53 in second innings, to become the only player to take 19 wickets in a Test. In all, Laker played in 46 Test matches and achieved a remarkable bowling average of 18.41.

CRICKET

When West Indian paceman Wes Hall first toured England in 1957, he had not taken a single first-class wicket. He made up for it in time.

New Zealand batsman Geoff Allott, batting against South Africa at Auckland in the 1998–99 Test series, was at the crease for 101 minutes. He was then out – for a duck.

Graham Gooch and Len Hutton both made ducks in their first Test innings.

On five separate occasions Ian Botham scored a century and took five wickets in an innings, during the same Test match. He reached 1,000 runs and 100 wickets in only his 21st Test.

The only Test batsman to have been out for a triple Nelson (333) is Graham Gooch. He made that total in the first innings of the Lord's Test against India in 1990. He then made a further 123 runs in the second innings, giving him an aggregate score of 456 – a world record for a Test match.

Pakistan's Zaheer Abbas scored 583 runs against India in 1978–79, at an average of 194.33.

Graham Gooch had made more than 1,000 Test runs before he scored a century. He didn't score a Test century until his 36th innings in 1980, but he went on to make another 19. In 1994, at the age of 41, he became the first batsman to score 2,000 runs on any Test ground – and he did it at Lord's.

Mike Gatting scored his first Test century in 1984. It was his 54th Test innings.

Cricketing Institutions:
Gentlemen v Players

The Gentlemen v Players game was a first-class cricket match played at least annually between a team of amateurs (the Gentlemen) and professionals (the Players). This custom began in 1806 and continued until the end of the 1962 season when the distinction between the two ended.

The fixture was played over three days, most commonly at Lord's, but also at a number of other grounds like the Oval and Scarborough. It was at Scarborough where the very last Gentlemen v Players game was staged in September 1962, the Players winning by seven wickets.

The same format was used in a number of other fixtures, some of which were given first-class status – for example, 'Gentlemen of Nottinghamshire v Players of Nottinghamshire' – but these became less common after the beginning of the 20th century.

CRICKET

A Man For All Seasons

With seasons of both sports extending to take up most of the year, the cricketing footballer is now a thing of the past. We look at one outstanding example, Chris Balderstone, who was cricketer, footballer and umpire, before remembering others of the now extinct breed later in the book.

An England international at cricket, Chris Balderstone played football for Carlisle and Doncaster. He made his debut for Yorkshire in the summer of 1961, moving to Leicestershire where his cricket career took off a decade later. He won the man of the match award in the Benson and Hedges Cup Final of 1972, and was awarded his County cap the following year. In 1976 he finally earned international recognition and faced the West Indies in the first Test, scoring 35 and four in his two innings, but was bowled out for 0 in both innings of his second Test appearance and was overlooked by England thereafter.

On 15 September 1975 he made sporting history when he rushed from Leicestershire's crucial County Championship match against Derbyshire at Chesterfield to turn out for Doncaster Rovers in their Fourth Division showdown with Brentford. Leicestershire went into their final game in search of the seven points which would guarantee them a first title. Doncaster were making headway in their bid to win promotion from Division Four.

At the end of day two, with Balderstone on 51 not out, he jumped into a taxi and was delivered to Belle Vue, where he helped Rovers battle out a 1–1 draw with Brentford. The next morning, he stepped back onto the cricket pitch to complete a century, his 116 helping Leicestershire to reach 260–6. With Balderstone taking three for 28, Derbyshire were bowled out for 140 with five minutes to spare, and the title was clinched.

No one had ever played first-class cricket and League football on the same day before, and no one ever will again. Balderstone retired from the playing side of cricket in 1986 and immediately qualified as an umpire, where he again made history by becoming the first ever third umpire to be used in a test match.

Don in the USA

Touring teams from the West Indies, England and Australia were playing in the USA and Canada until the 1920s. In one of the last such established tours before baseball took over, the Australian team played in Canada and the USA, leading to the naming of Stanley Park in Vancouver, British Columbia as Sir Donald Bradman's favourite cricket ground.

CRICKET

Great Batsmen I

'If ye Wicket is Bowled down, it's Out. If he strokes or treads down, or falls himself upon ye Wicket in striking, but not in over running, it's Out. A stroke or nip over or under his Batt, or upon his hands, but not arms, if ye Ball be held before she touches ye ground, though she be hug'd to the body, it's Out ...'

Extract from the Laws of Cricket 1744

JACK HOBBS

Jack Hobbs, the remarkable Surrey and England batsman, enjoyed a career which lasted from 1905 until 1934. Born in Cambridge in 1882, Hobbs played in 834 first-class matches, scoring 61,760 runs at an average of 50.70. In all, he made a total of 199 first-class centuries. In 61 Test matches, where he scored 5,410 runs at an average of 56.94, his opening partnerships with Yorkshire's Herbert Sutcliffe became the stuff of legend.

Hobbs was undoubtedly one of the finest batsmen of the twentieth century and, in 1953, he became the first professional cricketer to be knighted. He died in 1963.

DON BRADMAN

Born in 1908, Don Bradman went on to become the finest batsman ever to come out of Australia. There were far fewer Test matches in those days, but

Bradman's international career lasted from 1928 until 1948, and he made 6,996 runs in 52 Tests. This included two triple centuries, and a then record total of 334 in the Third Test at Headingley in 1930, when he was just twenty-one years old. Remarkably, 309 of those runs were scored in a single day.

When Don Bradman played his last Test innings, at The Oval in 1948, he needed just four runs for a remarkable Test match average of 100. Sadly for The Don, he was dismissed second ball by a googly from Eric Hollies, and he finished his international career with an average of 99.94. Sir Donald Bradman died in 2001.

LEN HUTTON

Len Hutton was born in Yorkshire in 1916 and went on to become another of England's finest batsmen. He made his first-class debut when he was 17 and his Test debut, versus New Zealand, when he was 21. He scored more than 40,000 first-class runs, played in 79 Test matches and had a Test average of 56.67. Hutton also bowled a bit, his leg-breaks earning him a total of 173 wickets.

Len Hutton's most famous achievement was his innings of 364, made against Australia at the Oval in 1938. The total was to stand as a record for many years. The England score of 903 for 7 has never been beaten. As well as Hutton's triple century, there were big hundreds from Maurice Leyland (187) and Joseph Hardstaff (169). England beat Australia by an innings and 579 runs. It seems a little unlikely that this will happen again.

Sir Leonard Hutton eventually moved south, and died in Kingston-upon-Thames, Surrey, in 1990.

Everyday Feats

Only five batsman in history have batted on all five days of a Test Match. They are:

M. Jaisimha, who scored 20 and 74 for India against Australia at Calcutta in 1959–60

G. Boycott, who scored 107 and 80 for England against Australia at Nottingham in 1977

K. J. Hughes, who scored 117 and 84 for Australia against England at Lords in 1980

A. J. J. Lamb, who scored 23 and 110 for England against the West Indies at Lords in 1984

R. J. Shastri, who scored 111 and 7 for India against England at Calcutta in 1984–85

In the Gloaming

At the Oval in August 1889, Surrey were playing Yorkshire. As the match drew to its close, the light became increasingly poor. Finally, gas-lamps were lit to provide some 19th-century floodlighting. The Surrey batsmen elected to continue with the innings, even though they could not see the deliveries of the Yorkshire fast bowlers, and could barely see each other. Finally, Surrey won the match by two wickets. One wonders what Dickie Bird would have done.

Cricketing Wit and Wisdom II

'Jason Gillespie is a thirty year-old in a thirty-six-year-old body.'

Bob Willis, during the 2005 Ashes series

'I doubt if many of my contemporaries, especially the older ones, did many exercises. I have often tried to picture Godfrey Evans and Dennis Compton doing press-ups out in the field before the day's play, but so far I've failed miserably.'

Peter May

'Cricket needs brightening up a bit. My solution is to let players drink at the beginning of the game, not after. It always works in our picnic matches.'

Paul Hogan

'Down the mine I dreamed of cricket. I bowled imaginary balls in the dark. I sent the stumps spinning and heard them rattling in the tunnels.'

Harold Larwood

CRICKET

'Oxford provided the perfect balance for me – to play top-class cricket as well as get a top-class education.'

Imran Khan

'You've come over at a very appropriate time; Ray Illingworth has just relieved himself at the Pavilion End.'

Brian Johnston

Keeping Good Company

Les Ames, the Kent and England wicketkeeper, took 79 catches and achieved 49 stumpings in 1929. Bob Taylor of Derbyshire and England took 1,473 catches and made 176 stumpings in a long and distinguished career which lasted from 1960 until 1988.

More Cricketing Brothers

New Zealand produced brothers Hedley **Howarth**, born in 1943, who played in 30 Tests and nine ODIs, and Geoff (1951) who played in 47 Tests and 70 ODIs.

Also from New Zealand came Jeff **Crowe**, born 1958, and his brother Martin (1962). Jeff played in 39 Tests and 75 ODIs, while Martin had 77 Tests and 143 ODIs to his credit.

In 1977 Leicestershire's Jeff **Tolchard** took over from his brother, Roger, as wicketkeeper in a match against

Derbyshire. Their nephew, Roger Twose, went on to play for New Zealand.

Graeme **Pollock** was born in Durban during 1944, and became one of the world's greatest left-handed batsmen. With South Africa exiled from world cricket at the time due to their unacceptable apartheid politics – he played comparatively few Test matches – just 23 in all – but his batting average was a staggering 60.97. Graeme's older brother Peter, born 1941, and a fast bowler, played in 28 Tests and had a bowling average of 24.18. Peter also produced son Shaun Pollock. Born in 1973, Shaun has more than a hundred Test matches to his credit, as well as almost 300 ODIs. A very straight bowler, he has a Test bowling average in the low twenties, as well as a batting average in the low thirties.

Andy **Flower**, who was born in Cape Town in 1968, is a fine wicketkeeper/batsman. He played in 63 Tests and 213 ODIs for Zimbabwe. His Test match batting average was 51.54. Andy retired from international cricket in 2003 after he and Henry Olonga bravely protested against the death of democracy in Zimbabwe. Andy's younger brother Grant played in 67 Tests and 219 ODIs. He too has retired from Test cricket, although his dispute with the Zimbabwean authorities, and the fact that he was a spokesman for the rebel players, more or less ensured that he would have to retire anyway. The brothers have both played County cricket for Essex.

CRICKET

Brothers Adam and Ben **Hollioake**, born in 1971 and 1972 respectively, both came from Melbourne but moved to England with their family in 1983. They both played for Surrey, and made half a dozen Test match appearances between them. Sadly, Ben died in March 2002 when, while back in Australia, he crashed his Porsche 968 into a wall in Perth.

Niall **O'Brien** was born in Dublin in 1981. He broke into the Kent side while their first-choice wicketkeeper, Geraint Jones, was in the England Test squad. Niall's brother Kevin, born Dublin in 1984, is a batsman who bowls a bit. Both played in the 2007 World Cup, Niall doing particularly well.

The O'Briens are very much a sporting family. Father Brendan played cricket for Ireland on 52 occasions, while sister Ciara has made more than a hundred appearances for the Irish women's hockey team.

It's Waugh!

The first batsman to have scored a hundred against all Test-playing countries is Steve Waugh. The Australian captain achieved this feat when he made 150 at Adelaide in December 1999. (At that point Bangladesh were yet to enter the Test arena.) Waugh added this century against India to seven against England, four against the West Indies, three each against Sri Lanka and Pakistan, two against South Africa and one each against New Zealand and Zimbabwe.

He was nearly beaten to the honour by his twin brother Mark, who was dismissed for 90 against Zimbabwe in Harare in the previous October.

The ECB (Gillette/NatWest/C&G/ Friends Provident) Trophy

English cricket's premier one-day tournament has borne many a name since it began life in 1963 as the One-Day Knockout Competition, sponsored by Gillette. It became the Gillette Cup the following summer, and the NatWest Trophy in 1981. It's said Gillette pulled out because folk identified them far more with cricket than razor blades.

The 20th and last final to be sponsored by the National Westminster bank was won by Gloucestershire, whose name – already engraved on the trophy in 1999 and 2000 – would remain there in the short term, regardless of how well they fared in the tournament, when it became the Cheltenham & Gloucester Trophy.

For a short period following the 2006 season, the competition was known as the ECB Trophy because no sponsors were forthcoming when Cheltenham & Gloucester decided to end their association. Friends

CRICKET

Provident are the current sponsors. The final takes place in August at Lord's.

Gamesmanship

It was said that W. G. Grace had a unique way of calling the toss. During Queen Victoria's reign, the penny showed her profile on one side and the figure of Britannia on the other. When the coin was tossed, W. G. offered a call of his own, which ensured that he always won. 'Woman', he is said to have called.

Famous Fans

When the Rolling Stones tour the globe, their contract rider spells out Sir Mick Jagger's needs. His vices might be limited these days to watching cricket, but promoters are required to provide cable or satellite access to televised matches. 'Please find out what channel is showing cricket. That is the channel we need most of all,' the document states. Mick apparently brings his own TV.

Sir Tim Rice, the Oscar-winning lyricist, is also a cricket lover and an accomplished author of such books as *The Treasures of Lords*, about the famous museum at London's Lord's cricket ground. He was President of the Marylebone Cricket Club in 2002, was Lord's Taverners president between 1988 and 1990, and is the prime mover of Heartaches Cricket Club.

Harold Pinter, the 2005 Nobel laureate, is a keen cricket fan – and actor Roger Lloyd Pack once said Pinter's writing could be compared with the sport. 'In both, there is a loving attention to detail and a formality, a passion and correctness – the same concentration,' he said. Pinter himself says: 'One's life has many compartments and I find cricket a wonderfully civilised act of warfare.'

Sir Paul Getty, the billionaire philanthropist, book collector and cricket lover, combined both his hobbies when he bought the company that publishes the *Wisden Cricketers' Almanack* in 1993. He remained chairman of John Wisden and Co. until his death in April 2003.

John Major, British Prime Minister from 1990 to 1997, has written books on cricket and was president of Surrey CCC until 2002. On his resignation from office he gave his final statement from Number Ten, in which he said, 'When the curtain falls, it is time to get off the stage.' Major then told the press that he intended to go to the Oval with his family to watch the cricket.

The Bunburys cricket team, founded by David English MBE, gives many cricket-loving celebs the chance to play in aid of charity. Their 2007 roll call included: ex-England rugby captain Martin Johnson, New Zealand all rounder Chris Cairns, Arsenal FC footballer and TV pundit Alan Smith, Brian Pieterson (brother of Kevin),

CRICKET

former footballer Micky Quinn, prime minister's son
James Major, former Stranglers frontman Hugh
Cornwell and one-time boxing champion Lloyd
Honeyghan.

All the Threes

Graham Gooch played in 118 Tests for England,
scoring 8,900 runs at an average of 42.58. He made 20
centuries, including his score of 333 against India at
Lord's in 1990.

Great Bowlers I

'Ye bowler must deliver ye Ball with one foot behind ye
Crease even with ye Wicket, and when he has bowled
one Ball or more shall bowl to ye number 4 before he
changes wickets, and he shall change but one in ye
same innings. He may order the Players that is in at his
Wicket to stand on which side of it he pleases at a
reasonable distance …'

Extract from the Laws of Cricket 1744

FRED TRUEMAN
'He just loved to bowl. You gave him the ball, he
wanted to bowl. He got through 1,100 overs on average
a year: many, many more than players do nowadays,
and people of his era tell amazing stories of his stamina
and will to win.'

This was Ian Botham's comment on Fred Trueman, who was born in Stainton in the West Riding of Yorkshire in February 1931. Rumour has it that he weighed more than 14lb at birth. Fast bowler Trueman soon grew up, and made his debut for his beloved Yorkshire in 1949. He went on to play in 67 Tests and take 307 wickets at an average of 21.57. His first-class average was 18.29.

'Fiery Fred', as Trueman was popularly known, was probably the first English sledger, as he would frequently intimidate batsmen with a bit of down-to-earth black Yorkshire humour accompanied by a cold stare. He might well have played in rather more Test matches, had it not been for his somewhat aggressive attitude towards the cricket authorities. Cricket authorities tend not to like players speaking their minds.

Trueman went on to become a caustic summariser on radio's *Test Match Special*, his dismay at certain aspects of the modern game being summed up by one of his more frequent comments: 'I don't know what's going off out there.' Fred Trueman died in July 2006.

DEREK UNDERWOOD
Born in 1945, Derek Underwood was one of Kent's finest bowlers. He was a left-arm orthodox spinner, although he was quicker than most spin bowlers and often bowled at medium pace. Underwood made his

debut for Kent in 1963 at the age of 17, and soon became known as 'Deadly'. He was deadly indeed, on rain-affected wickets. Deadly Derek went on to feature in 86 Test matches and 26 ODIs. He took 297 Test wickets at an average of 25.83.

Perhaps his most famous performance came in the Fifth Test against Australia in 1968. On the final day, a thunderstorm sent the players dashing for the pavilion. Play resumed with only about half an hour left and a draw seemed inevitable, but Underwood took advantage of the earlier downpour and removed four Australian batsmen in 27 balls. Deadly's feat meant that, instead of losing the Ashes series 1–0, England had squared it.

BISHAN BEDI

Bishan Bedi, a slow left-arm bowler, was born in 1946. He played 67 Test matches for India and had an excellent bowling average of 28.71. He also played County cricket for Northamptonshire for many years.

Bedi has always been something of a controversial and outspoken character. As captain of India during a series in the West Indies in 1976, he complained of intimidatory tactics and declared his side's innings closed after two players had retired hurt. He became coach of the Indian national side in 1990 and, after India had played badly on one tour, he threatened to dump the entire party in the sea on the return journey.

He did not remain coach for very long. Bishan Bedi has likened the bowling action of Muttiah Muralitharan to a javelin throw and, although the Sri Lankan spinner's action has been officially cleared by the cricket authorities, Bedi believes it constitutes cheating.

Snow Joke!

In June 1975, Derbyshire played Lancashire at Buxton. Lancashire batted first and scored 477–5 declared on the first day, before taking two quick Derbyshire wickets. On the second day, a Monday, no play was possible due to there being an inch of snow on the pitch. Umpire Dickie Bird opined that he had 'never seen owt like it' which was reasonable enough. To the surprise of many, the wicket was considered fit for play on the Tuesday: Derbyshire were soon all out for 42 and then, following on, were all out again for 87.

Little Big Man

Kent and England's Alfred Percy Freeman – better known as 'Titch' because he stood at just 5 feet 2 inches – took 304 first-class wickets in 1928, at an average of 18.05. In 1930 he took 275 wickets at 16.84, in 1931 276 at 15.60, and in 1933 he took 298 at 15.26. Titch Freeman played for England only a dozen times, always saving his best performances for his beloved Kent.

CRICKET

Talking Cricket II

CHINAMAN

An off-break, bowled by a left-arm bowler to a right-handed batsman, is known as a Chinaman. The origin of the term is uncertain, but it may have come from a West Indian player of Chinese descent who first employed this type of delivery in the 1930s.

DOOSRA

The term 'doosra' has come into fashion in recent years. In the Asian languages Hindi and Urdu, the word means 'other' or 'second'. In cricket it is used to describe a ball bowled by an off-spin bowler which actually turns from leg to off. In a sense, it is the off-spinner's version of the googly. The rather strange action employed by such players as Muttiah Muralitharan in delivering the doosra has been questioned by many. It has, however, been officially declared to be legal.

DUCK

No, a duck is not eaten with orange sauce the night before a match. If it is, then it's tempting providence. A duck in cricket is a score of nought. The term 'golden duck' is applied when a batsman is out for nought first ball, 'a pair' is a duck scored in each innings, and a 'golden pair' is likely to lead to a batsman being punched on the nose by his captain.

DUCKWORTH/LEWIS METHOD

This is a rather complicated mathematical formula used for deciding on the number of runs needed to win by the side batting second in a one-day match which has been interrupted by bad weather. Calculations are made regarding the number of overs left to play, and the number of wickets to have fallen. The system was devised by Frank Duckworth and Tony Lewis, and nobody really understands it – least of all commentators, who tend to nod sagely and tell everyone that the method works really well most of the time.

FULL TOSS

A full toss is a ball which reaches the batsman without pitching. Bowlers often deliver full tosses when they are attempting to bowl a 'Yorker' and batsmen often dispatch them gleefully to the boundary.

Old Campaigner

In 1976, the 45-year-old Brian Close was called up for the first three Tests in England's five-Test series against the West Indies. In the second innings of the third Test at Old Trafford, Close's final Test knock, he opened with the 39-year-old John Edrich against Michael Holding, Andy Roberts and Wayne Daniel.

It was with this innings of 20 runs off 108 balls in 162 minutes against bowling Wisden described as 'frequently too wild and hostile to be acceptable' that Close completed his Test career. The interval between first and last Test matches was 27 years, the second longest after Wilfred Rhodes. Only one man, Zimbabwean John Traicos, has played a Test match at a greater age since.

Test Grounds of the World I

Brisbane Cricket Ground is known as **The Gabba** because of its Woolloongabba location. It is home to both the Queensland cricket team and the Brisbane Lions Aussie Rules side and has been used for baseball, cycling, Rugby Union and athletics.

At the Western Australia Cricket Association Ground (**WACA**) in 2003, Australia's Matthew Hayden made a massive 380 against Zimbabwe, which constituted a Test record at the time. The same venue saw Dennis Lillee introduce his infamous aluminium bat in 1979 – an incident that would be hard to beat in headline-grabbing terms. And let's not forget Glenn McGrath's 300th Test wicket against the West Indies in 2000, when he completed a hat-trick in the process.

Ian Botham seemed to relish playing in Mumbai's **Wankhede Stadium**; his century and 13 wickets in the Jubilee Test of 1980 was one of his best single-match hauls – and even though England lost the Test there the following year, he still managed a nine-wicket total. Botham would definitely have approved when a few years later Ravi Shastri, playing on the same ground, hit six sixes in an over on his way to a fastest ever first-class double century.

The **Eden Gardens** cricket ground is to India what Lord's is to England and the MCG Australia. This is a huge venue that sprung from recreational land presented to the people of Calcutta by the governor-general back in the 19th century. The influential Calcutta Cricket Club soon established itself at Eden Gardens and the first pavilion was built in 1871. Eden Gardens is an intimidating place for visiting players and supporters alike and even more so when home support gets totally out of control as it has in the past; a World Cup semi-final in 1996 had to be abandoned due to unruly crowd behaviour.

The Test record of the **Kotla** in Delhi started in November 1948 when the visiting West Indies amassed a score of over 600 (four batsman scoring centuries) but India still managed to squeeze out a draw. Four years later Pakistan were defeated by an innings to give the home side a first win at the venue.

Thereafter India only tasted victory twice out of nineteen games played up until their 1993 win over Zimbabwe. Happier times were to come, however, for the Zimbabwe game, which featured a double-century from Vinod Kambli, heralding a run of five victories including the toppling of both Australia and Pakistan.

County Championship

The birth of the County Championship occurred in 1890, when a meeting determined conditions of play, points scored and Counties contesting the title. Founder members were Gloucestershire, Kent, Lancashire, Middlesex, Nottinghamshire, Surrey, Sussex and Yorkshire.

Somerset were included in 1891, while Derbyshire, Essex, Hampshire, Leicestershire and Warwickshire joined four years later. Worcestershire (1899), North-amptonshire (1905) and Glamorgan (1921) were latecomers.

While rules and regulations have chopped and changed, these counties remained constant until the 1992 admission of Durham. In 2000, to encourage excitement and eliminate too many meaningless late-season games, the Championship was split into two divisions of nine teams, each playing 16 matches. The first promotions and relegations took place at the end of the season, though three up/three down was reduced to two up/two down in 2006.

Walsh Woe

West Indian fast bowler Courtney Walsh holds the dubious distinction of having registered a record number of 43 ducks in 128 Test matches. He did however retire from Test cricket in 2001 as the first and only man to take 500 wickets at the highest level.

Highs and Lows

Highest County Championship team scores:

887	Yorkshire v Warwickshire, Edgbaston, 1896
863	Lancashire v Surrey, The Oval, 1990
850–7d	Somerset v Middlesex, Taunton, 2007
811	Surrey v Somerset, The Oval, 1899
810–4d	Warwickshire v Durham, Edgbaston, 1994
803–4d	Kent v Essex, Old County Ground, Brentwood, 1934
801–8d	Derbyshire v Somerset, County Ground, Taunton, 2007

Lowest County Championship team scores:

12	Northamptonshire v Gloucestershire, Spa Ground, Gloucester, 1907
13	Nottinghamshire v Yorkshire, Trent Bridge, 1901
14	Surrey v Essex, County Ground, Chelmsford, 1983
15	Hampshire v Warwickshire, Edgbaston, 1922
16	Warwickshire v Kent, Angel Ground, Tonbridge 1913

CRICKET

20 Sussex v Yorkshire, The Circle, Hull, 1922
20 Derbyshire v Yorkshire, Bramall Lane, Sheffield, 1939

Women's Cricket

'The greatest cricket match that was played in this part
of England was on Friday, the 26th of last month, on
Gosden Common, near Guildford, between eleven
maids of Bramley and eleven maids of Hambledon, all
dressed in white. The Bramley maids had blue ribbons
and the Hambledon maids red ribbons on their heads.
The Bramley girls got 119 notches and the Hambledon
girls 127. There was of bothe sexes the greatest number
that ever was seen on such an occasion. The girls
bowled, batted, ran and catched as well as most men
could do in that game.'

The *Reading Mercury* report of 26 July 1745 describes the
first recorded women's cricket match in England. The
next game took place almost exactly two years later
between the women of Charlton and those of Westdean
and Chilgrove, Sussex. This had to be finished the
following day because of crowd trouble!

Women's cricket had been played since the turn of the
20th century in Australia. In Britain, the Women's
Cricket Association (WCA) was established in 1926 by a
group of enthusiasts who adopted MCC laws and ran
matches throughout the country. In their first season

the WCA staged 49 games and established a popular cricket festival which still runs today at Colwall Cricket Club, Herefordshire.

England played their first game against The Rest at Leicester in 1933, the first international tour, to Australia, taking place a year later. England won two tests and drew one, then went on to New Zealand where Betty Snowball scored 189 in the first ever Test between the two countries. Australia first visited the UK in 1937; the honours were shared with a draw at the Oval and a win apiece.

The first women's World Cup in 1973 saw England, prompted by captain Rachael Heyhoe-Flint, beat Australia in the final by 92 runs. History was again made three years later when the first-ever women's Test was held at Lord's featuring the same teams.

Dickie Bird umpired at the third Women's World Cup, held in New Zealand in 1982 and won by Australia, and was 'most impressed by the overall standard'. Each of the 14 English players had to contribute £250 towards travelling costs.

Today women's international cricket is played by eleven countries, with seven playing Test matches of more than one day. Originally three-day matches, most of these have been played over four days since 1985.

CRICKET

In 1998 the Women's Cricket Association voted to merge with the ECB, thus becoming part of a single governing body which controls cricket in the UK.

Ten-Wicket Haul

Having taken 10 for 36 the previous summer against Warwickshire, Yorkshire and England's Hedley Verity took 10 for 10 in 19.4 overs, with a quite remarkable 16 maidens, against Nottinghamshire in 1932. Verity died aged 38 in 1943, as a result of wounds received in action during the Second World War.

Initial Success

Kent and England's Colin Cowdrey was actually christened Michael Colin Cowdrey, because has father was determined he would play for the MCC.

Priced Out

Barbados spent 30 million US dollars on the re-development of the Kensington Oval in Bridgetown, in time for the 2007 World Cup. The other Caribbean nations also invested in ground improvements and it was money well spent, as they looked magnificent. Unfortunately though, in order to claw back some of the money, the authorities charged far too much for entry to the one-day games. Most of the locals could not afford the inflated prices, and many matches were very poorly attended. With the World Cup games being spread over what was generally considered to be too long a period, the whole enterprise was not the success which had been hoped for. Australia won it, too.

Steely Resolve

Bespectacled Northamptonshire batsman David Steele came late to Test cricket. The silver haired, serious-looking cricketer was 33 when first selected to play for his country, against Australia in 1975. He was, though, rather less than serious in real life. For his benefit season, he persuaded a Northampton butcher to sponsor him by way of the promise of gifts of meat. The butcher reputedly ended up owing him 1,756 lamb chops – one for every run Steele scored that summer.

Cricketing Wit and Wisdom III

'A cricket ground is a flat piece of earth with some buildings around it.'

Richie Benaud

'Geoffrey is the only fellow I've met who fell in love with himself at an early age and has remained faithful ever since.'

Dennis Lillee, speaking about his old mate Geoff Boycott

CRICKET

'I know why he's bought a house by the sea: so he'll be able to go for a morning walk on water.'
Fred Trueman commenting on former team-mate Geoff Boycott's house move from Yorkshire to Poole Harbour

'When you win the toss – bat. If you are in doubt, think about it – then bat. If you have very big doubts, consult a colleague – then bat.'

W. G. Grace

'England have only three major problems. They can't bat, they can't bowl and they can't field.'

Martin Johnson

'I have on occasion taken a quite reasonable dislike to the Australians.'

Ted Dexter

'Shane Warne's idea of a balanced diet is a cheeseburger in each hand.'

Ian Healy

Cricketing Institutions

WISDEN
The sport's definitive record, the *Almanack Of Cricket*, took its nickname from John Wisden, a diminutive (5ft 4in) fast bowler nicknamed the 'Little Wonder'. A new edition of Wisden has been published every year since

1864, the first priced at one shilling. The famous yellow cover first appeared on the 75th edition in 1938.

The most famous copy of Wisden belonged to writer E. W. 'Jim' Swanton, who had it with him when he was taken prisoner by the Japanese and lent it to cricket-starved fellow prisoners like a library book. This well-thumbed edition is now in the museum at Lord's.

In Wisden's centenary year of 1963, a full set of Almanacks in good condition was said to be worth £250. Nowadays a full set would cost well in excess of £30,000.

LORD'S

Yorkshireman Thomas Lord came south to London and set up a cricket club in 1787, and this became known as Marylebone Cricket Club (MCC) The first match at Lord's was MCC versus Hertfordshire, played on 22nd June 1814. MCC bought the freehold of the ground in 1866. The first Test match at Lord's took place in 1884, when England met Australia and (amazingly) won the match by an innings and five runs.

When Lord established the ground named after him in St John's Wood, London, he could scarcely have realised that, close to two hundred years later, Lord's would still be regarded as both the headquarters of the game and most revered of cricketing venues. That a

structure built in the same century as the ground's
opening would still take centre stage would also have
been unimaginable. The structure concerned is the
pavilion. Built in 1890, it is flanked on one side by the
Warner Stand dating from 1958 and, on the other, by
the less imposing Allen Stand.

Lord's is the home of Middlesex County Cricket Club.
By tradition, the second Test of a series is played at the
home of English cricket, although in recent years the
number of Tests played during a summer has led to
this being varied.

THE OVAL
London's other Test match ground is The Oval, home
of Surrey CCC. A cricket club treasurer called William
Baker took out a lease on some ground which was
being used as a market garden, at the Oval,
Kennington. He laid a cricket pitch consisting of turf
from Tooting Common and the Oval, as we know it,
was born.

In August 1845 the Gentlemen of Surrey met the
Players of Surrey in a match, and not long afterwards
Surrey CCC was formed. For many years the Oval was
used for other sports – notably soccer and rugby – but
by 1895 it was decided that too much damage was
being done to the turf (hardly surprising) and from then
on few football matches took place there. In more

recent years though, the Oval has been used for pop concerts. The first Test match to be played there began on 6th September 1880. Incredibly, England beat Australia by five wickets.

The Oval did not have a pavilion until 1858 – this had to serve the club for 40 years before another took shape. The long-established Vauxhall Stand was joined in the 1980s by three more constructions, named after Surrey stalwarts Bedser, Lock and Laker. Just as Lord's is traditionally the venue for the second Test, so the Oval is traditionally the venue for the final Test of a series.

TRENT BRIDGE

The Trent Bridge ground was originally in the back garden of a pub. Admittedly, it was a very large garden, belonging as it did to one William Clarke, landlord of the Trent Bridge Inn. Clarke was the captain of the Nottinghamshire County side, and he constructed the cricket ground in 1838. Two years later, the first first-class match was played there. The first Test to be played at Trent Bridge was England v Australia in June 1899 – the result being a draw.

From the 1860s, Nottinghamshire County Cricket Club shared the facilities with Notts County Football Club who did not move on until 1910; it was then felt that, with Test cricket having already been introduced to the ground in 1899, the two sports could no longer co-habit.

EDGBASTON

Warwickshire County Cricket Club needed a ground and so William Ansell, their honorary secretary, helped find a suitable site in Edgbaston, Birmingham. The ground was constructed by 1886, and its first match, played in June of that year, was Warwickshire v MCC. The first Test match took place in May 1902, when the Australians were all out for 36, but bad weather eventually forced a draw. After another match against Australia in 1909 (in which the Aussies were all out for 74) Edgbaston was not used for Test matches for many years. It became a regular Test venue after 1957.

Further development did not take place until the 1990s when the input of lottery money allowed the Eric Hollies Stand, the Edgbaston Cricket Centre and a cricket shop to be added to established structures like the R. E. S. Wyatt, William Ansell and Raglan Stands. In 2005 discussions began with regard to the possibility of Warwickshire County Cricket Club joining Birmingham City Football Club at a new stadium which would house 50,000 all-seated spectators.

OLD TRAFFORD

Old Trafford came into being in 1857 and has been the home of Lancashire County Cricket Club since 1864.

In June 1865, Lancashire first played another county – Middlesex – on the ground. 1884 saw the first Test match played at the ground, and also saw the start of its reputation for attracting rain. The first day of Old Trafford's very first Test against Australia was washed out. Neither this, nor the fact that the ground was bombed during the Second World War, prevented Old Trafford from becoming a regular Test venue to this day.

No Test match has been more breathtaking than the 1956 fourth Ashes Test when England's Jim Laker spun the home side to victory. In Australia's first innings, he returned figures of 9 for 37 and followed it up with 10 for 53 in the second. Unsurprisingly, these combined bowling figures have never been bettered in international cricket.

In terms of drama packed into the first over of the day, little could top Dominic Cork's Sunday morning charge as he bagged a hat-trick against the West Indies in 1995.

HEADINGLEY
In 1887 the Leeds Cricket, Football and Athletic Company Ltd, under the chairmanship of Lord Hawke, bought a 22-acre site to use as a sports field. It was divided into portions, and cricket was first played there in 1890. A year later Yorkshire County Cricket Club

played its first first-class game at Headingley, and Test cricket followed in 1899.

Yorkshire County Cricket Club only acquired ownership of their home ground in 2005 after a tie-up with Leeds Metropolitan University and a loan from Leeds City Council. In future the ground will be called the Headingley Carnegie Stadium, thanks to a huge redevelopment involving Leeds Rhinos Rugby League team and their Rugby Union counterparts the Tykes.

Until these latest moves, the future of Headingley as a Test Match venue was in doubt. It is unthinkable that a ground that has witnessed such events as two triple centuries from Don Bradman, John Edrich's triple in 1965, Boycott's achievements before his own crowd and the epic 1981 Test, when Botham and Willis contrived to snatch victory from nowhere, should be relegated to non-international status.

RIVERSIDE

Just as Durham is the newest of the first-class counties, so their Riverside Ground, at Chester le Street, is the newest of this country's Test match venues. Durham were granted first-class status in 1991, and they moved into their new headquarters four years later, their first County Championship match being against Warwickshire in May 1995. Prior to this momentous event, Durham had existed as a minor county since 1882.

The Riverside hosted some World Cup matches in 1999, and has been the venue for other ODIs. Although it now has Test match status, it has so far been used very infrequently. In June 2003, the Riverside became the first new Test venue in over 100 years when Zimbabwe were England's opponents. England bowler Richard Johnson took 6 for 33 in Zimbabwe's first innings during that first Test. There are surely many more memorable moments to come.

Arms and the Man

Hanif Mohammad, normally a right-arm bowler, changed to his left arm in the middle of an over whilst he was playing for Pakistan against Somerset in 1954 – and took a wicket with the left-arm delivery.

Classy Clive

Clive Lloyd took the wicket of M. J. K. (Mike) Smith with his first ball in a one-day international.

Cricket and the Media: Radio

The BBC's *Test Match Special* has provided ball-by-ball commentary of England matches since 1957. The first BBC radio commentary at Leyton, some 30 years earlier, was promoted with the slogan: 'Don't miss a ball, we broadcast them all.'

CRICKET

The 1970s found master commentators John Arlott and Brian Johnston developing their own style, discussion continuing even when there was no play. Statistician Bill Frindall encouraged interest in the figures of the game.

After 30 years on Radio 3, the programme's future was uncertain as the 1990s approached. However, Radio 4 stepped in as its saviour and in 1994 the broadcasting team settled into its now familiar position on 198 metres Long Wave.

TMS has also become available in the current millennium via digital channel Five Live Sports Extra. Current mainstays include former England fast bowler Jonathan Agnew and Christopher Martin-Jenkins, one of the few survivors (with Henry Blofeld) from the old days. Many overseas guests play their part: Alan McGilvray from Australia (since succeeded by Neville Oliver) and Barbadian Tony Cozier between them entertained British listeners for over half a century, while in 1998 in Trinidad, *Test Match Special* employed its first female commentator, Barbadian Donna Symmonds.

Many spectators at Test matches listen to *TMS* via headphones attached to portable radios, and there is occasionally 'dialogue' between the commentators and those present at the ground. A large number of television viewers watch the action on their TV sets with the sound muted and *TMS* commentary turned up.

Four the Match

In Baroda, India in 1947, there was a remarkable fourth-wicket partnership of 577 between Gui Mahomed and Vijay Hazare of Baroda, playing against Holkar for the Ranji Trophy. Baroda scored 784 in their first innings, and won the match by an innings and 409 runs.

On the Farm

During 1887 a village team from Yatton, near Bristol, took on a team consisting of up to fifty farmers. Forty-one of the farmers actually batted, but many of them failed to score and their final total was just 92 (for 40). Yatton made 75–6 in reply, so the match was presumably drawn. Had Henry Blofeld been present, he would have had a great deal of fun describing the field whilst Yatton were batting.

School Daze

A report in Wisden of the annual Eton v Harrow cricket match in 1872 revealed that 'Never before was congregated on Lord's Ground so numerous and brilliant a company …' and 'The crush at the gates on the first day was great and lasting beyond all precedent …' An unthinkable happening today for a meeting of the two public schools, but symptomatic of how popular organised cricket was when still in its relative infancy – and how passionate a following it could create.

Twin Spirits

J. S. (Jack) and his identical twin W. H. **Denton** opened the innings together for Northamptonshire in the 1914 season. They were so alike that the scorer had a very tough time working out who had scored what.

Twins Sidney and Dudley **Rippon** were amateur batsmen who played for Somerset whenever they could. Sidney worked for the Inland Revenue and for one game, in 1919, he was unable to get time off to play. So he went sick, and played for the county under his grandmother's name – S. Trimnell. Unfortunately, he did rather well, making 92 and 58 not out against local rivals Gloucestershire. Who was this Trimnell, everyone asked? As some 9,000 spectators had watched him bat, it was quite hard to keep his real identity a secret for long, and it was eventually revealed. Apparently, the Revenue saw the funny side of it all, and forgave him. They probably made him pay tax on his match fee, though.

Steve **Waugh**, born in 1965, made 168 Test appearances for Australia between 1985 and 2002. A fine batsman, he averaged 51.06. He also played in 325 ODIs, but his twin brother, Mark, was even more famous. Mark was a great stroke player who featured in 128 Tests between 1991 and 2002, and had a batting average of 41.81. He also played in 244 ODIs.

The most famous twins of all were Alec and Eric **Bedser**, who were born in Reading, Berkshire, in 1918. Both played County cricket for Surrey, and Alec was the more accomplished of the two. He bowled accurate, right-arm medium-fast deliveries off a short run, and his inswingers and leg-cutters were remarkably accurate. In 1953, at the age of 35, Alec took 39 wickets at an average of 17.48, as England won the Ashes. In all he made 51 Test appearances, and had a bowling average of 24.89. His first-class average was 20.41.

Eric, a bowler of off-breaks and a right-handed batsman, played first-class cricket from 1939 until 1962, making more than 450 appearances. He died, aged 87, in May 2006. The twins were remarkably close and did almost everything in tandem. In 1957, County Champions Surrey awarded each of them £15 worth of Premium Bonds. Thirty-five years later, two buff envelopes arrived by the same post. Each contained a £50 prize, one for Alec and one for Eric: this was one of the many coincidences that occurred throughout their lives.

CRICKET

George is Innocent!

During the Third Test match against Australia at Headingley in 1975, the wicket was damaged overnight by protesters claiming that one George Davis was innocent of a crime for which he was doing time. Amongst other damage, oil was poured onto the wicket, and the match had to be abandoned. George Davis was eventually released, but he was soon back inside for another crime – one that he admitted having committed.

Luck of the Irish

Most people were pleased when Ireland did so well in the early stages of the 2007 World Cup, and qualified for the Super Eights. It couldn't last, however. When the Irish (one or two of whom were actually Australian) met the Aussies at the later stage, they were dismissed for a paltry 91 runs, and lost the match by nine wickets. Later still, in their final match, they made just 77, with Sri Lanka winning by eight wickets.

Named and Shamed?

Almost every part of the Kensington Oval in Barbados is now named after a famous Barbadian player. It seems unlikely that many members of England's current side will be remembered in this sort of way.

For the Record: Test Matches II

W. G. Grace was the oldest Test match captain. He last skippered the England side in 1899, when he was almost 51. Mark Greatbatch, the large New Zealand batsman, played the part of W. G. Grace in a feature film. Unfortunately, Greatbatch was left-handed, so the film had to be reversed.

In a Test in Johannesburg in 1995, England wicketkeeper Jack Russell was responsible for 11 dismissals.

Chris Broad made six Test centuries for England, but none of them were scored on home territory.

India and Pakistan have held each other to a 0–0 draw in Test match series on three occasions.

Australia had gone 18 Test matches without a draw, until they came upon the might of the English weather in the Second Test at Lord's in 1997. No play was possible on the first day due to rain, and the match eventually ended without result.

The flamboyant Godfrey Evans wasn't always flamboyant at the crease: in a Test match against Australia in 1947, he took 97 minutes to get off the mark.

CRICKET

Pakistan first played a Test series against India in 1952–53. They first won one in 1978–79.

Trevor 'Barnacle' Bailey took 357 minutes to score a half-century in Brisbane during 1958–59.

Imtiaz Ahmed played in each of Pakistan's first 39 Test matches between 1952 and 1962.

In 1912 a series of three-day tests was organised in England, the participants being the home nation, Australia and South Africa. The tournament was no great success, but there was some joy for the Australian leg-spinner Jimmy Matthews when his team played South Africa in Manchester. Matthews took a hat-trick in each innings, but he failed to achieve greater fame as he was to play in only eight Tests in his entire career.

England have twice beaten Australia having followed on. They did it in 1894 and, rather more famously, they did it again in 1981.

Out on a Limb

A couple of hundred years ago, soldiers and sailors frequently returned from the wars with body parts missing. They still wanted to play sport of course and, although attitudes to disability were very different then, matches featuring players with missing limbs became very popular. There was too, a good deal of betting on them. In 1796, Aram's New Ground, Montpelier Gardens, Walworth hosted a game between the Greenwich Pensioners with one arm, and the Greenwich Pensioners with one leg. The two-inning match commenced on 9th August, and was played over two days. The One Legs won by 103 runs.

The Greenwich (naval) Pensioners were particularly fond of amputee cricket. In a match played in Camberwell on 25th August 1841, Greenwich Pensioners took on the Army Pensioners of Chelsea (i.e. the Chelsea Pensioners). Every player had either an arm or a leg missing, but the Chelsea side was older and was well beaten. In another match during the 1840s, a batsman's wooden leg came off while he was taking a run. He managed to hop to the other end, but a one-armed fielder picked up the wooden leg and threw it at the stumps before the batsman had made his ground. The umpire decided that the one-legged batsman had been legally run-out. This decision would appear to have been somewhat harsh.

Over the Top

Prior to 1835, only under-arm bowling was permitted. Round-arm bowling, where the ball is delivered from around shoulder height was then made legal. There were, however, moves afoot to make over-arm bowling legal too, and in August 1862 at the Oval, matters came to a head. Surrey were playing All-England and a Surrey bowler, one Edgar Willsher, decided he would cause a bit of trouble by bowling over-arm. Umpire John Lillywhite was not amused, and proceeded to no-ball him six times. Willsher, plus the other professionals in the side, then walked off, to the undoubted consternation of all concerned. The match continued the next day, umpire Lillywhite having decided to withdraw gracefully, and within two years MCC decided to make over-arm bowling legal.

The Nearly Men

The County Championship could have been 20 counties, not 18. An invitation to Buckinghamshire was declined in 1921, due to lack of proper playing facilities, and an application by Devon in 1948 was rejected.

Tree's Company

Quite a few village cricket grounds have trees within their boundaries. The most famous tree however, was that growing gracefully at the St Lawrence Ground, Canterbury – the home of Kent County Cricket Club. Depending on which wicket was in use, this lime tree was often within the playing area, and four runs were scored whenever it was struck. Sadly, the Canterbury

Lime was coming to the end of its long innings and had to be felled a couple of years ago. Bits of it are on sale in the club shop, and a new lime tree has now been planted.

Cricketing Institutions: the MCC

Founded in 1787, the Marylebone Cricket Club – better known throughout the cricket world as the MCC – is the world's most famous cricket club. It is based at Lord's.

In 1788, it laid down a Code of Laws requiring the wickets to be pitched 22 yards apart and detailing how players could be given out. Its Laws were adopted throughout the game, and it today remains the custodian and arbiter of how cricket is played around the world.

At the turn of the century, the Board of Control for Test Matches, the Advisory County Cricket Committee and the Imperial Cricket Conference were all set up to cater for the growth in domestic, imperial and other international cricket. These bodies existed until 1968 when there was a major reorganisation of cricket in England. Since the MCC was a private club it could not receive public funds, so it set up a Cricket Council as the governing body of cricket and the Test and County Cricket Board to administer the professional game. It also converted its MCC Cricket Association into the National Cricket Association to look after the recreational game. As a result, cricket started to receive financial help from the government.

In the 1990s, the structure was changed again with the England & Wales Cricket Board (ECB) taking over responsibility for all cricket in England from the TCCB, NCA and Cricket Council.

The MCC's role has continued to evolve in response to these changes. Today, its key responsibilities include: ensuring that Lord's remains a ground which is world-class, as well as world-famous; promoting cricket's Laws and safeguarding its 'spirit'; promoting cricket to young people, for the long-term good of the game; helping to increase cricket's international appeal – not least through its teams' touring programmes; and maintaining its position as the world's most active cricket-playing club.

Cricketing Wit and Wisdom IV

'You might remember me. I was captain of England when they were crap.'
    Nasser Hussain, speaking at the British Asian Awards

'Many Continentals think life is a game. The English think cricket is a game.'

George Mikes

'The other advantage England have got when Phil Tufnell is bowling is that he isn't fielding.'

Ian Chappell

'I feel I have had a very interesting life, but I'm rather hoping there is still more to come. I still haven't captained the England cricket team.'

Jeffrey Archer

'Cricket makes no sense to me. I find it beautiful to watch and I like that they break for tea. That's very cool, but I don't understand. My friends from The Clash tried to explain it years and years ago but I didn't understand what they were talking about.'

Jim Jarmusch

'Cricket to us was more than play. It was worship in the summer sun.'

Edmund Blunden

Behind the Stumps

During the Oval Test in 1884, England wicketkeeper Alfred Lyttelton took off his pads and, as a bowler, took 4 for 19 for his side against Australia. Meanwhile, in

CRICKET

1893, Gloucestershire wicketkeeper W. H. Brain stumped three Somerset batsmen in successive deliveries – a very rare example of a hat-trick of stumpings.

In 1901, the Oxford University wicketkeeper was injured in a match against Somerset. It was then agreed between the two captains that the Somerset wicketkeeper, the Rev A. P. Wickham, should keep for both sides. When he batted, one wonders whether he attempted to stump himself.

Grave Rumour

The pitch at the national stadium of Grenada, in the West Indies, used to be so dead it was rumoured that its turf came from the nearby graveyard.

Till Death Us Do Part

When he died, Henry Bagshaw, an umpire from 1907 until 1923 who had previously played for Derbyshire, was buried in his umpire's coat. A ball was also placed in his hand.

England Test match bowler Alfred Shaw wanted to be buried near to his Nottinghamshire and England compatriot, Arthur Shrewsbury. He got his wish, and was buried 27 yards from Arthur – the length of the pitch, plus five yards for Alfred's run up.

Double Trouble

Arthur Fagg created a remarkable record in 1938.
Batting for Kent against Essex at Colchester, he scored
two double centuries – 244 in the first innings, and 202
not out in the second. The 244 included a century
before lunch on the first day.

World Cup

The Cricket World Cup is held (roughly) every four
years and is said to be the world's third largest and
most viewed sporting event. The first international ODI
championship was held in England in 1975, as were the
following two events. (The winner of one year now
becomes the host country of the next.) The tournament
was officially known as the Prudential Cup in its early
days after the sponsors, Prudential plc.

The finals are contested by all ten Test-playing nations,
together with six others that qualify through the World
Cup Qualifier. The 2007 tournament began with a pool
stage, played in round-robin format, followed by a
'Super 8' stage, semi-finals and a final. Australia
defeated Sri Lanka to retain the trophy.

Seven teams have competed in every tournament, five
of which have won the trophy. Australia has won four,
the West Indies won the first two tournaments, and

CRICKET

India, Pakistan and Sri Lanka have each won once.
The West Indies (1975 and 1979) and Australia (1999,
2003 and 2007) are the only nations to have won
consecutive titles.

World Cup Winners
1975	West Indies
1979	West Indies
1983	India
1987	Australia
1992	Pakistan
1996	Sri Lanka
1999	Australia
2003	Australia
2007	Australia

The Under-Achievers

The four current first-class counties yet to win a County
Championship title are Durham, Gloucestershire,
Northamptonshire and Somerset. Since 1895,
Derbyshire have finished bottom on 14 occasions.

Alight Entertainment

In 1884 the England party that toured Australia
comprised smokers and non-smokers in more or less
equal proportions. At the end of the tour it was decided
that a match between the smokers and non-smokers

should be arranged, with some Aussies included to make up the numbers. Various companies put up prizes of cigars for the smoking side. The non-smokers however made 803 in their only innings, whilst the smokers made a gasping 356 and 135–5. The match was thereby drawn. But the smokers had surely proved to the as yet unborn fathers of the nanny state that smoking is bad for you.

Great All-Rounders

'If in running a notch ye Wicket is struck down by a throw, before his foot hand or Batt is over ye popping crease, or a stump hit by ye Ball though ye Bail was down, it's Out. But if ye Bail is down before, he that catches ye Ball must strike a Stump out of ye ground, Ball in hand, then it's Out.'

Extract from the Laws of Cricket 1744

GARFIELD SOBERS

Garry Sobers was probably the closest anyone has been to becoming the perfect cricketer. Born in Barbados in 1936, he had an extra finger on each hand which was removed at birth. An excellent all-round sportsman, Sobers was a left-handed batsman, a slow left-arm bowler and also a left-arm fast-medium bowler.

He played in his first Test match in 1953 at the age of 17. Five years later, he scored 365 runs in a Test innings against Pakistan. This was a new world record, and it stood until it was surpassed by Brian Lara 36 years later. Remarkably, it was Sobers' maiden Test century. Altogether he was to play in 93 Tests, scoring 8,032 runs at an average of 57.78. He took 235 Test wickets at 34.03. As well as all this, Sobers was an excellent close fielder. It's hardly surprising that the West Indies were so hard to beat while he was playing.

Sobers played County cricket for Nottinghamshire. In 1968, playing against Glamorgan at Swansea, he hit Malcolm Nash for six sixes in one over. Garfield Sobers became Sir Garfield in 1975 and was created a National Hero of Barbados in 1999.

RICHARD HADLEE

Born in Christchurch, New Zealand, in 1951, Richard Hadlee played cricket for Canterbury Cricket Club (NZ), Nottinghamshire and, of course, New Zealand. Given the name of his first club, he should really have played County cricket for Kent. Hadlee was a bowling all-rounder, but he was in fact one of the best bowlers of all time. He was a left-handed batsman, and a right-arm fast bowler – his most deadly ball being the outswinger, which he developed later in his career.

Richard Hadlee played in 86 Test matches, taking 431 wickets at an average of 22.29. In those games he scored 3,124 runs at an average of 27.16. In ODIs his bowling average was slightly better – 21.56, while his batting average was 21.61. When New Zealand toured Australia in 1985, Hadlee took a total of 15 wickets in the Brisbane Test. The Kiwis won by an innings. In 1990 he became the first bowler in the world to take 400 Test wickets and, in the same year, was knighted for his services to cricket.

IAN BOTHAM

Ian Botham was born in Heswall, Cheshire, in 1955. For a time he was a professional footballer with Scunthorpe United, but it is of course as a cricketer that he is remembered. He was an attacking batsman and a right-arm fast-medium swing bowler, although back trouble forced him to reduce his pace in the latter part of his career. He played for Somerset between 1974 and 1985, but left that county in protest at the sacking of his mates, Viv Richards and Joel Garner. He then played for Worcestershire, and later Durham.

In 1980, against India, Ian Botham became the first player to score a century and take ten wickets in a Test match. In all, he featured in 102 Tests and had a batting average of 33.54. He also took 383 Test wickets, at an average of 28.4. The averages are not perhaps as wonderful as you might expect, but Botham did put in some marvellous displays and he became every schoolboy's hero. He captained England on 12 occasions, but his captaincy was not marked with success. Altogether Ian Botham scored almost 20,000 runs in first-class cricket, and took 1,172 wickets. He also held 354 catches.

Ian Botham took 383 Test wickets for England, at an average of 28.40.

A Commons Lot

At East Grinstead in Sussex during September 1955, a team of politicians played a Stage XI in aid of the Sackville College Appeal. Harold MacMillan, then Foreign Secretary, and later to become Prime Minister, played for the Politicians. He was out hit-wicket for 2, off the bowling of Richard Hearne (a children's comedian, known as Dr Pastry). Rex Harrison played for the Stage XI, and he was out for a duck. A few professionals were included on both sides, including Denis Compton who, somewhat strangely, was also out for a duck. The match ended in a draw, with the Politicians having made 178 and the Stage 162–8.

Ump got it Wrong

Umpires have long been criticised for the making of bad decisions, although it is generally recognised that their job is a remarkably tough one. Usually, dodgy decisions are simply debatable, but occasionally it's totally obvious that an umpire has got it wrong. Apart from decisions as to whether or not a batsman is out, there are examples of umpires not paying proper attention to who is bowling. In 1921, in a Test match against England, Australian captain Warwick Armstrong bowled the last over before rain stopped play, and was then allowed to bowl the next over when play restarted. Thirty years later New Zealand bowler Alex Moir was permitted to bowl consecutive overs before and after tea in a Test versus England, in Wellington.

Meanwhile, during the World Cup in 1983, West Indian batsman Viv Richards returned to his crease after a break for bad light – except that it wasn't his crease. He had returned to the wrong end, but was still allowed to take strike.

Yanks a Lot!

The USA sent touring cricket sides abroad in the 19th century. It achieved its greatest success when a national side defeated the West Indies by nine wickets in an international match in British Guyana in the 1880s.

Small Scores

In May 1872, MCC played Surrey on an appalling wicket at Lord's. The first day was lost to rain, and the match finally started just after noon on the second day. MCC batted first – and W. G. Grace was out for a duck. He was not alone. Seven other batsmen also scored the dreaded zero, and at one stage the MCC score was 0–7. A rally followed, and the final total was 16 all out. Surrey did rather better in their first innings, notching up a score of 49, before MCC batted again, and made the magnificent total of 71 (Grace 11). Surrey then made 39–5 to win the game by five wickets, at 6.40pm on the same day.

With Thanks to the Sponsors

The County Championship has had six sponsors since 1977:

Schweppes (1977–1983)
Britannic Assurance (1984–1998)
PPP Healthcare (1999–2000)
Cricinfo (2001)
Frizzell (2002–2005)
Liverpool Victoria (2006–present)

Good Grace!

Jim Laker may have taken 19 for 90 against Australia in 1956, but in 1907 Colin Blythe of Kent took 17 for 48 in a match against Northamptonshire at Northampton, while in 1877 W. G. Grace took 17 for 89 for Gloucestershire against Nottinghamshire at Cheltenham.

Test Cricket

The word Test applies to matches played between national teams that represent the ultimate test of sporting ability. Sports such as rugby union, rugby league, netball and hockey have used the term, but there is no doubt that it most famously applies to cricket.

Though the term Test match was first used to describe an English team that toured Australia in 1861–62, the first ever official Test match commenced on 15th March 1877 and was contested by England and Australia at Melbourne Cricket Ground, where the Australians won by 45 runs.

Nations seeking Test status apply to the International Cricket Council, whose decision is based on that nation's performance in matches against fellow Associate Members of the ICC and against Test match nations. The level of organisation of cricket and the existence of development programmes for the sport will also be taken into account.

The face of world cricket is changing, and there has been an expansion of cricket into countries that were never part of the British Empire. Countries such as Argentina, Holland and the Arab Emirates are now able to play in world cricket, and this may well be the biggest change that has occurred in the sport in modern times. They are represented by the International Cricket Conference, whose ICC World Cup Qualifier (formerly ICC Trophy) is an international one-day cricket tournament whose top six qualify for the Cricket World Cup.

The ten official Test nations:

England (first Test 1877)
Australia (1877)
South Africa (1889)
West Indies (1928)
New Zealand (1930)
India (1932)
Pakistan (1952)
Sri Lanka (1982)
Zimbabwe (1992)
Bangladesh (2000)

A Major Talent?

Former Prime Minister John Major wrote the following Cricket Prayer in a boring Commons moment:

Oh, Lord, if I must die today,
Please make it after close of play.
For this I know, if nothing more,
I will not go, without the score.

411 for Four

In 1957 Peter May and Colin Cowdrey put on a Test record 411 runs for the fourth wicket, against the West Indies at Edgbaston.

Quake Awake!

Whilst the West Indies were playing India in a one-day international at the Queen's Park Oval, Trinidad, in 1983, an earthquake stopped play. It was a fairly short-lived tremor and no players were injured. Several spectators were, however, hurt when they leapt from the stands, thinking they might collapse.

Freddie Afloat

England all-rounder Andrew Flintoff became the first test cricketer to be found drunk in charge of a pedalo in March 2007. He had to be rescued from the Caribbean at 4am on a Saturday following a drunken night out. The fact that the night out took place within 36 hours of England's World Cup meeting with Canada did not go down well with the England management, and he was dropped and stripped of the England vice-captaincy. With untypical understatement, 'Freddie' said he was 'upset and embarrassed'.

CRICKET

For the Record: County Cricket I

'It would be impossible to lay down any cast-iron
reason for the fact that general interest in cricket has
increased by leaps and bounds in the last twenty years.
The fact is incontrovertible, whatever the cause may be,
but to most of those who have watched the course of
cricket events, the progress of County cricket will
present itself as the primary cause of the progress of the
game as a whole.'

W. J. Ford, writing a little over a hundred years ago

The County game is the basis of professional cricket in
England and Wales, and long may it continue to be so.
Here are a few snippets concerning this remarkable
competition.

Derbyshire lost 17 out of their 18 County Championship
matches in 1920. The other one ended in a draw.

Paul Collingwood took a wicket for Durham with his
first ball in first-class cricket. He also scored 91 in the
same match.

Northamptonshire were all out for 12 in a match
against Gloucestershire in 1907.

In 1991 Essex won six of their last seven matches to
clinch the County Championship.

Jack Russell, later to be a distinguished England wicketkeeper, became Gloucestershire's youngest ever 'keeper when he made his debut at the age of 17. He was still at school, and he probably wore a very battered school cap.

Kent failed to win the County Championship between the wars, yet they finished in the top five places on 16 occasions.

In the Pink

Middlesex played their 2007 Twenty20 campaign in a unique pink kit to promote the Breakthrough Breast Cancer charity. For every replica of Middlesex's Twenty20 shirt, male and female design, and cap sold, a donation of £5 and £2 respectively was made to Breakthrough Breast Cancer.

Cricket and the Media: Television

England's home Test matches were the sole province of the BBC until 1999, when Channel 4 outbid them. In 2006 the England and Wales Cricket Board awarded an exclusive four-year contract to satellite broadcaster BSkyB. The deal was reportedly worth £220m, a 10% increase in real terms on the previous agreements.

Highlights of each day's play in the Test matches were,

however, screened on Five, which replaced Channel 4 as cricket's sole terrestrial broadcaster. The BBC retained exclusive rights for radio coverage of home Tests and one-day internationals.

There was controversy when Channel 4 ended the BBC's 61-year tenure of screening England's home Test matches. Former England captain Alec Stewart was one of many who felt it would have a detrimental effect on the game: 'Young girls and boys should be able to see cricket without having to pay for it. The ECB have to look at the whole picture. They may be getting a big cheque but, long-term, English cricket will suffer.'

Channel 4, in fairness, added much to televised cricket's analysis, with clever camera angles and quirky graphics. BBC commentators Richie Benaud and Geoff Boycott were signed up, and the result was not displeasing. Then came the BSkyB deal, meaning that for the first time in history, live coverage of England's home Test matches was no longer available on terrestrial TV.

Cricketing Wit and Wisdom V

'Sometimes I think I had the best of both worlds, sometimes the worst. What I should really have done was played golf!'

Footballing cricketer Chris Balderstone

'I became a professional cricket teacher about twenty years ago. I had a son born to me when I was fifty, and I thought, he needs someone to bowl to him.'

Peter O'Toole

'He charmed the crowds by the way he used to wave his bat. He just captivated them.'

Colin Cowdrey on Denis Compton

'I hate losing, and cricket being my first love, once I enter the ground it's a different zone altogether, and that hunger for winning is always there.'

Sachin Tendulkar

'You can cut the tension with a cricket stump.'

Murray Walker

'Geez. I just played cricket because I loved the game. I never thought about it much; never had any formal coaching.'

Steve Waugh of Australia

Irish Eyes

Irish cricket came to prominence during the 2007 World Cup, but the game has been played on the Emerald Isle for a very long time. As far back as the 1830s, Horace Rochford, a slow left-arm bowler, was one of its pioneers. Horace did, however, have a most peculiar action. His run-up was quite long for a slow bowler, but during it Horace would stop several times, hold the ball close to one eye, and squint at it. Exactly why he did this, no one ever knew.

Golden Oldies

William Lillywhite, one of the first round-arm bowlers, was 61 years old when he opened the bowling for Sussex against England in 1853. William Quaife played his last County Championship match for Warwickshire in 1928, when he was 56 years old. The game was against Derbyshire, and this William scored 115 in his only innings.

B & H Reunion

The umpires in the last ever Benson & Hedges Cup final, John Hampshire and Barry Dudleston, had faced each other as players in the first final on the same Lord's pitch 30 years before.

Watching and Wasting

Cricket can be a costly business. In India, losses to the economy from cricket watching were recently estimated at $10 billion a year. Cricinfo, the world's largest single-sport website, has pointed out that cricket on the net is just making the problem worse. 'Cricket is ideally suited to Internet coverage as it is a game that is played during working hours and it is a game that involves a wide range of statistics.' Even if companies block access to cricket websites, satellite TV and mobile phone services now provide updates for the dedicated.

Cricket in the Big Apple

The first annual Canada v USA cricket match, played in 1844, was attended by 10,000 spectators at Bloomingdale Park in New York. This fixture is claimed by some to be the oldest international sporting event in the modern world, predating even today's Olympic Games by nearly 50 years.

Mighty Comeback

In 1922, Hampshire were all out for 15 in their first innings against Warwickshire at Edgbaston. However, they did rather better in their second innings, scoring 521 – and amazingly went on to win the match by 155 runs.

For the Record: Test Matches III

Norman Oldfield would seem to be England's unluckiest 'one-Test wonder'. In his only game, in 1939 against the West Indies, he made 99 runs – 80 of them in his first innings.

CRICKET

Batsman Frank Woolley of Kent became the oldest wicketkeeper in any Test match when he deputised for Les Ames, also of Kent, in a Test against Australia in 1934. Woolley was 47.

Jonathan Agnew, now a well known and very good radio commentator, took just four Test wickets for 373 runs – an average of 93.25. Poor old Aggers.

In 66 Test innings, Mike Brearley averaged only 22.88 and never scored a century. He did however have a remarkably good record as the England captain, and was widely regarded as one of the most intuitive and clear-thinking captains of all time.

Anil Dalpat was the first Hindu to play Test cricket for Pakistan – in 1984.

Yorkshire's Geoff Boycott featured in 108 Tests, scoring 8,114 runs at an average of 47.72. In all, he spent more than 450 hours at the crease. And he never got bored once.

West Indies fast bowler Michael Holding scored 22.5% – nearly a quarter – of his 910 Test match runs in sixes.

In 1997 the first West Indies v England Test, at Kingston, Jamaica, was abandoned after just 62 balls had been bowled. England were 17–3 at the time.

At the age of 22, New Zealand's Glenn Turner became the youngest batsman to carry his bat (remain undefeated throughout the innings) in a Test match. He did it at Lord's in 1969. Having made just five in the first innings, he was 43 not out in the second, when his side was dismissed for 131.

Sri Lanka scored a massive 952–6 dec in the First Test against India in 1997–98.

In 1955, while playing against India, Maqsood Ahmed of Pakistan became the first player to be stumped for 99 in a Test match.

Sunil Gavaskar played in 106 consecutive Tests. However, his run ended in 1987 when he refused to play in Calcutta because spectators had been having a go at him.

Ton Up Both

In 1985, Ian Botham became the first player to complete the double of 1,000 runs and 100 wickets in one-day internationals.

First-ball Fun

Indian left-arm spinner Nilesh Kulkarni dismissed Marvan Atapattu with his first ball in Test cricket, at

CRICKET

Colombo's Premadasa Stadium in the 1997–98 season, and then bowled 419 more balls without success.

'Each Umpire is ye sole judge of all Nips and Catches, Ins and Outs, good or bad Runs, at his own wicket, and his determination shall be absolute, and he shall not be changed for another Umpire without ye consent of both Sides. When ye four Balls are bowled he is to call Over.'

Extract from the Laws of Cricket 1744

Few umpires can probably claim to be loved by one and all but, unlike many football referees, they do generally command the respect of players and, in some cases, they really are loved. Here are one or two of the better-known umpires from recent years.

England's **Dickie Bird**, born in 1933, the son of a Barnsley coal miner, was eventually to become the most famous of the modern-day umpires. He was to stand in 66 Tests and 69 ODIs. His sense of humour and at times eccentric behaviour helped him in the popularity stakes, as did the fact that he was clearly an emotional man. Together with Michael Parkinson, he very nearly turned the Yorkshire town of Barnsley into a popular tourist destination. Nearly, but not quite. Dickie Bird's last Test match was in 1996, and he stood in his last County game a couple of years later. He cried a lot when he finally stood down.

One of the marvellous things about cricket is that fat blokes can often play it very well. **David Shepherd**, born in Bideford, Devon in 1940, was a roundly built and very popular cricketer, who came quite late into the County game with Gloucestershire. When he hung up his batting gloves, he turned to umpiring, and became even more popular as a County and international official between 1981 and 2005. One of David Shepherd's little foibles was that he would hop about on one leg whenever the scoreboard showed the dreaded Nelson – a score of 111. Well, why not?

David Constant, born in Wiltshire during 1941, is included here entirely because of his name. Indeed, what more appropriate surname could an umpire have? And Dr Constant was indeed constant. He became a Test match umpire at the tender age of 29 and went on to stand in 36 Tests. He spent almost 38 years umpiring in the County Championship.

Talking Cricket III

GOOGLY
The googly or 'wrong 'un' is a ball bowled by a right-arm bowler with a leg-break action, which is actually

an off-break. It is bowled from the back of the hand and, if the batsman fails to pick it up, the googly may well result in the slow walk back to the pavilion.

LBW

This is Leg Before Wicket – one way in which a batsman may be out. If, when a ball is bowled, it strikes the batsman's leg and would, in the opinion of the umpire, have gone on to strike the wicket, then the batsman may be given out. There are however various rules which apply to this type of dismissal and in some cases the batsman should be given not out, even when the ball would have struck the stumps. Together with catches taken behind the wicket, when the bat may or may not have just grazed the ball, LBW is by far the most contentious of the methods of dismissal.

MAIDEN OVER

A maiden over is one in which no runs are scored. Bowlers love to bowl a maiden over, and many do it even when they're not playing cricket.

NIGHT-WATCHMAN

A night-watchman may be employed to prevent the pitch from being vandalised overnight. This however is quite unusual. More usually, he is a lower-order batsman who comes in to bat shortly before close of play, in order to save a specialist batsman from having to risk losing his wicket during the last few balls of the day.

NO-BALL

A no-ball is a delivery which the umpire deems to be illegal. It may be called for a number of reasons, including the bowler's front foot being 'over the line'. One run – an 'extra' – is normally added to the total of the batting side when a no-ball is called, and the ball is bowled again. In other words, if one no-ball is bowled during the course of a six-ball over, then seven balls will actually be bowled. Runs may be scored freely from no-balls and the only way a batsman may be out to such a delivery is if he is run out.

RETIRED HURT

A batsman who is injured during the course of his innings may be forced to retire hurt. He may, however, return to the crease at the subsequent fall of a wicket, should he be physically able to do so.

Great Batsmen II

JAVED MIANDAD

Javed Miandad was born in Karachi in 1957. Widely regarded as Pakistan's greatest ever batsman, he played for his country between 1975 and 1996. During his long career he made 8,832 runs in 124 Test matches (189 innings) at an average of 52.57. His highest score was 280 not out, in a Test against India. Although not a regular bowler, he took 17 Test wickets with his leg spinners.

CRICKET

Miandad was also a great one-day batsman, playing in 233 one-day internationals (ODIs) and scoring another 7,381 runs. During 1987–88 he scored back to back fifties in ODIs – a world record. He was never out for a duck in Pakistan in Tests or one-day games.

DAVID GOWER

David Gower was born on 1st April 1957 in Tunbridge Wells, Kent, although he never played for that county. He was educated at King's School, Canterbury and at University College, London and, as a left-handed batsman, he went on to play for Hampshire, Leicestershire and England.

Gower was a very stylish cricketer, to whom batting appeared to come easily. Although he often seemed to get himself out just when it seemed that a great innings was imminent, he nevertheless scored 8,231 runs in 117 Test matches between 1978 and 1992, and had a batting average of 44.25. He also played in 114 ODIs, scoring a further 3,170 runs at an average of 30.77. His captaincy of the England side initially met with success, but his seemingly casual approach did not go down well with everyone. Since retiring from playing, David Gower has become a stylish commentator on the game.

BRIAN LARA

A tremendous hitter of the ball, left-handed batsman Brian Lara (known to his many fans as the Prince of

Port of Spain) was born in Trinidad in 1969. A naturally gifted player, he has played some quite phenomenal innings in his time. Whilst playing County cricket in England, he made an astonishing 501 not out for Warwickshire in a game against Durham in 1994. The innings lasted for 474 minutes, Lara facing 427 deliveries and scoring ten sixes and 62 fours.

Brian Lara also scored 400 not out for the West Indies against England in a Test match in Antigua in 2004. The West Indies made 751 for 5, but the match was drawn. Although there was never any doubting his brilliance as a batsman, Brian Lara, and his captaincy of the West Indies side, came in for a good deal of criticism over the years. He has now retired from international cricket.

Balloon Stopped Play

Some years ago, an umpire in Sri Lanka had something of a surprise when a large fish fell from the sky and landed at his feet. This is not an everyday occurrence, even in Sri Lanka. It turned out that a sea eagle, harassed by a flock of crows, had dropped its lunch.

Mind you, the fish was nothing compared to the hot-air balloon which landed in the middle of a village cricket pitch near Southampton in 1982. The balloon had run out of fuel and its pilot had been forced to make an emergency landing. While the players endeavoured to remove the debris from the pitch, the scorer duly recorded 'Balloon Stopped Play' in the scorebook.

Great Wicketkeepers

'Ye Wicket Keepers shall stand at a reasonable distance behind ye wicket, and shall not move till ye Ball is out of ye Bowler's hand, and shall not by any noise incommode ye Striker, and if his hands, knees foot or head be over or before ye Wicket, though ye Ball hit it, it shall not be Out.'

Extract from the Laws of Cricket 1744

GODFREY EVANS

Born in 1920, Godfrey Evans made his debut for Kent in 1939, just before the start of the Second World War. He was to become the finest wicketkeeper in the world; squat and sturdy, with amazingly quick reactions. He was a flamboyant character, and his off-field antics would have made tabloid headlines today. Evans played in 91 Test matches between 1946 and 1959. He was responsible for 219 dismissals, and was the first wicketkeeper to reach the 200 mark. He was able to bat defensively, but his batting was inclined to be as flashy as his 'keeping. He had a Test average of 20.49.

In 1967, eight years after his official retirement and at the age of 46, Godfrey Evans again turned out for his county: Alan Knott was playing in a Test match and Kent had no second 'keeper available. Needless to say, Evans kept beautifully. After retirement, Godfrey Evans became cricket 'expert' for bookmakers Ladbrokes. He was very keen, but perhaps a little naive. When, in the Headingley Test against Australia in 1981, England were asked to follow on 227 runs behind, he persuaded Ladbrokes to offer odds of 500–1 on an England victory. Ian Botham and Bob Willis then conjured up a remarkable win for the home side.

When he was awarded the CBE, Godfrey Evans proudly stated that it stood for Crumpet Before Evensong. He died in 1999, and is sadly missed.

RODNEY MARSH

Rod Marsh was born in Perth in 1947. He played for Western Australia and for the Australian Test side, for whom he turned out on 96 occasions. In all, he took 343 Test match catches, and executed 12 stumpings. More than a quarter of his dismissals came from the bowling of Dennis Lillee. An accomplished batsman, Marsh scored three Test centuries, and had a Test match batting average of 26.51. His 92 ODI games saw him average 20.08.

Marsh was one of the first and worst sledgers. He had presumably not read the bit in the Laws which states that a wicketkeeper 'shall not by any noise incommode ye Striker'. Rod Marsh played hard and drank hard, and he would not have lasted five minutes under the cricket regimes of today. He was Australian through and through, although some years after his retirement in 1984 he became, for a few years, an England selector.

ALEC STEWART

Born in Merton, Surrey, during 1963, Alec Stewart was a fine wicketkeeper/batsman. He made his debut for Surrey in 1981 and played Test cricket from 1990 until his retirement in 2003. He began his career as a specialist batsman who kept wicket occasionally. The sometime England captain made a massive 133 Test match appearances, scoring 8,463 runs at an average of 39.54. When in the side as a batsman only – frequently as an opener – his average was in the high forties. During the 1990s he shared England wicketkeeping duties with Jack Russell, but still claimed a total of 277 victims from behind the stumps. In 170 ODIs Stewart scored a further 4,677 runs at an average of 31.6. He also took 159 catches and made 15 stumpings.

Alec Steward had a great batting technique. He was especially adept at dealing with pace bowling, and his cover drives were something to behold. His highest Test score was 190, against Pakistan in the first Test at Edgbaston in 1992.

The National League

Currently sponsored by NatWest as the Pro40 League, this began in 1999, and was essentially the old Sunday League which had existed for 30 years. Its new title reflected the fact that many matches were now played on days other than weekends.

The first-class counties are divided into two divisions, with teams promoted and relegated from each. Currently, a play-off game is held between the teams third from top in the second division and third from bottom in the first. The competition is played over 40 overs per side, each county playing the other once.

Counties have been encouraged to incorporate nicknames into their official names for the National League.

Derbyshire Phantoms
Durham Dynamos
Essex Eagles
Glamorgan Dragons
Gloucestershire Gladiators
Hampshire Hawks
Kent Spitfires
Lancashire Lightning
Leicestershire Foxes
Middlesex Crusaders

CRICKET

Northamptonshire Steelbacks
Nottinghamshire Outlaws
Somerset Sabres
Surrey Brown Caps
Sussex Sharks
Warwickshire Bears
Worcestershire Royals
Yorkshire Phoenix

Thousand Apologies

During the 1922–23 Australian season, the Victorian State side scored 1,059 in their first innings against Tasmania. They went on to win the match by an innings and 666 runs. Four years later Victoria were again causing the scoreboard operator to wonder what to do because he only had space for three numbers, when they once more made over a thousand runs in an innings – this time scoring 1,107 against New South Wales.

Men for all Seasons:
more Cricketer-Footballers

Ian Botham managed 11 appearances (seven starts) as a non-contract player for Scunthorpe United between 1979 and 1984, a time when he was also hitting all-comers out of the ground for both Somerset and England. And he's still vice-president of the Iron.

Denis Compton not only represented Arsenal and England on the football field, picking up an FA Cup winner's medal with Arsenal in 1950, but also spent 22 years with Middlesex, amassing 78 Test caps in the process. Brother Leslie followed in the same vein with Middlesex (though not for his country), while also forging a career with the Gunners and winning two England football caps.

Worcestershire skipper Phil Neale was probably the last true professional cricket and football player, although his football career was spent in the lower leagues with Lincoln.

Viv Richards may be the only man to represent his country in both soccer and cricket World Cup competitions, playing for Antigua in qualification. Richards was once dismissed by Coventry goalkeeper Steve Ogrizovic when Ogrizovic (of Shropshire) played for the Minor Counties against the touring West Indies.

Until his death on 25th April 2007, at the age of 79, Arthur Milton was the last surviving player to be capped for England at both cricket and football. Like the Compton brothers, he played for Arsenal, and he played in just one England international – against Austria in 1951. Milton was a very good batsman and a fine slip, and short-leg, fielder for Gloucestershire, representing that county until he was well into his forties. He featured in six Test matches and in his first, at Headingley against New Zealand in 1958, he scored 104 not out.

Like Milton, Willie Watson (Sunderland/Yorkshire) both represented England at football and cricket in the 1950s. Team-mates of Milton at Gloucestershire who also played football included Harold Jarman (Bristol Rovers), Bobby Etheridge and David Smith. At Yorkshire, Watson was joined by Ken Taylor, who was a regular for Huddersfield Town.

Brian Close of Yorkshire and England played football as an amateur for Leeds United and became the first Leeds player to play international football at youth level when in October 1948 he played for England against Scotland.

At the end of National Service in October 1951, he signed for Arsenal, and tried to combine this with his cricket for Yorkshire. But it proved impossible: Close received permission from Yorkshire captain Norman Yardley to leave the first match of the 1952 cricket season but this leave of absence was later rescinded in Yardley's absence. Close arrived late at Arsenal and was sacked. Close played for Bradford City in 1952, but whilst doing this picked up a serious knee injury that ended his professional footballing career.

Jim Standen won an FA Cup winner's medal for West Ham in 1964, and played in the Worcestershire team that won the County Championship in 1964 and 1965 (he topped the national bowling averages in one season). Ted Hemmings was in the same Worcestershire squad as Standen, and also turned out at wing-half for Shrewsbury Town. The Hammers also had Eddie Presland, who played cricket over several seasons for Essex. And Geoff Hurst, apparently a wicketkeeper, also played at least once for the Essex first XI.

Noel Cantwell (West Ham, Man Utd) played football and cricket for Ireland, while Andy Goram (Oldham Athletic, Rangers, Hibernian) did the same for Scotland. He kept wicket for Scotland against the Australians in 1989, but when Rangers learned of this they banned him from playing cricket in case of injury.

Graham Cross represented Leicester City during the winter and Leicestershire CCC during the summer during the 60s and 70s. Present-day footballer Phil Neville of Everton once captained England's U15 cricket team and even represented Lancashire's second string.

C. B. Fry played in the 1902 FA Cup final for Southampton, and for England v Ireland in 1901, as well as playing 26 cricket Tests for England, holding a long-jump record that stood for 21 years, and famously being offered the throne of Albania!

CRICKET

In 1958, England's opening pair in the third Test against New Zealand at Headingley was Arthur Milton, the Gloucestershire batsman and Arsenal winger who played one full international for England (against Austria in October 1951), and Warwickshire's Mike Smith, who won one rugby cap as England's fly-half against Wales in 1956.

Good Grace?

It is perhaps a little surprising that W. G. Grace, whose career ran from 1865 until 1908, played in 869 first-class matches, scored 54,211 runs ... but only averaged 39.45. Could it be that the great man was not quite as good as he thought he was?

Three-sy Does It!

Sri Lankan left-arm seamer Nuwan Zoysa holds the record of taking a hat-trick from the first three balls he bowled in a Test match. In only his eighth Test, Zoysa achieved this against Zimbabwe at Harare in November 1999. In his first three balls he took the wickets of Trevor Gripper, Murray Goodwin and Neil Johnson.

Missing the Boat

The last, and longest, of the so called 'Timeless Tests' took place in Durban during March 1939. The idea was, of course, that the timeless nature of the match would ensure that a result would be forthcoming. This particular encounter was eventually to last for ten days. There was a fair amount of bad weather, but in all 43 hours of cricket were played. MCC (England) and South Africa scored a total of 1,981 runs between them – but the match still ended in a draw. It would have gone on for longer, but had it done so the MCC players would have missed the boat home. Oh dear.

Big Hitters

Most runs against another team in one County Championship season.

547	W. G. Grace, Gloucestershire v Sussex, 1896
537	M. R. Ramprakash, Surrey v Northamptonshire, 2006
534	G. Boycott, Yorkshire v Nottinghamshire, 1983
531	C. B. Fry, Sussex v Nottinghamshire, 1905
527	R. M. Poore, Hampshire v Somerset, 1899
526	J. G. Langridge, Sussex v Derbyshire, 1949
507	H. Sutcliffe, Yorkshire v Essex, 1932
502	C. Washbrook, Lancashire v Sussex, 1947
501	B. C. Lara, Warwickshire v Durham, 1994

Test Series

Test matches are played in series between two nations that can range from one to six matches. Every match in a scheduled series is played, even if one side gains an unbeatable lead.

The International Cricket Council (ICC) has compiled the results of home and away series between pairs of nations to calculate relative rankings in an official World Test Championship table.

Traditional rivals such as England and Australia play two series every four years, one in each country; others play at less regular intervals. The ICC is in the process of instituting a rotation system in which each pair of nations plays home and away series at least once per five years.

Definition of a Test match

A Test match is a game of two innings for each side, played over five days, of six hours' play each. Each day of play consists of three two-hour sessions of play – the morning, afternoon and evening sessions. These are divided by a 40-minute interval for lunch, and a 20-minute interval for tea.

Additionally, the players take a 10-minute interval at the change of an innings, unless the innings ends within ten minutes of a scheduled interval or the end of play.

Test matches are played over five consecutive days, though they have occasionally included a rest day after the third or fourth day of play. Playing hours are scheduled for daylight only.

Cricketing Wit and Wisdom VI

'Our absolute and complete affinity is hard to explain but it is true and very real to us – so much so that as long as I can remember, we have never been happy apart'.

> Sir Alec Bedser, speaking of his relationship with his identical twin Eric

'Fast bowlers are quick. Just watch this. Admittedly it's in slow motion.'

> Ian Chappell

'It is amazing how the public steadfastly refuse to attend the third day of a match, when so often the last day produces the best and most exciting cricket.'

> Frank Woolley, speaking when County Championship games were spread over three, rather than four, days

'Cricket civilises people and creates good gentlemen. I want everyone to play cricket in Zimbabwe; I want ours to be a nation of gentlemen.'

> Robert Mugabe. Yes, he really did say it.

'Cricket is not a thrilling and exciting game all the time. You couldn't have a match which goes on for five days, six hours per day, thrilling and exciting every minute. It's essentially a situation game and it's the situation which creates the excitement, not television.'

> Trevor Bailey, taking issue with a TV
> executive's assertion that cricket was a
> 'thrilling and exciting game'.

President's Choice

The first cricket clubs in the USA were established in the 1700s, not long after they made their first appearance in England, and were populated by officers of the British Army and local landed gentry. Several Founding Fathers of the United States were known to be avid cricketers – one, John Adams, stated in the US Congress in the 1780s that if leaders of cricket clubs could be called 'presidents' there was no reason why the leader of the new nation could not be called the same!

Cold Cricket

Cricket matches on ice took place in this country in the 19th century, even though our climate was seldom really suitable. Ice cricket is however quite popular in some Scandinavian countries and now in Tallinn, Estonia, there is even an annual ice cricket tournament which features amateur cricketers from the United Kingdom. It takes all sorts – especially in Estonia.

Great Bowlers II

DENNIS LILLEE

Dennis Lillee was one of Australia's greatest ever fast bowlers. He was born in Perth, Western Australia in 1949, and he made his Test match debut against England at Adelaide in 1971. He went on to play in a total of 70 Tests, taking an incredible 355 wickets at an average of 23.92. He was also to feature in 63 ODIs and achieve an average of 20.82.

From the mid-1970s Lillee bowled in partnership with another excellent paceman, Jeff Thomson, thus leading to confusion amongst less well-informed listeners to radio commentaries, when they thought they heard the likes of Brian Johnston refer to one 'Lillian Thomson'. Spinal stress fractures almost brought a premature end to Dennis Lillee's career, but he fought back and was able to carry on playing in Test matches until 1984.

MALCOLM MARSHALL

Born in Bridgetown, Barbados in 1958, Malcolm Marshall was initially taught to play cricket by his grandfather. The boy grew up to be just five feet eleven inches tall, which is quite short for a fast bowler. A fast bowler he was, though, and he went on to play in 81 Tests and take 376 wickets, at a remarkable average of 20.94. His ODI average was 26.96. Marshall was very nearly an all-rounder, as he normally came in at Number 8 and had a Test batting average of 18.85.

Having broken a thumb whilst fielding in the first innings, he proceeded to take 7 for 53 in England's second innings during the Headingley Test in 1984. He also took 7 for 22 in the Old Trafford Test in 1988, although this was against a very indifferent – not to say bad – England batting line-up. Much loved and respected at Hampshire, where he played County cricket, Malcolm Marshall died of cancer in 1999, at the tragically early age of 41.

SHANE WARNE

Shane Warne was born in 1969. A right-arm leg-break bowler of exceptional ability, he was to play for Australia in 145 Test matches and 194 ODIs. He retired from Test cricket in January 2007, having taken 708 wickets at an average of 25.41. He took ten wickets in a Test match on no less than ten occasions, and his ODI bowling average was 25.73.

Warne, who has had a colourful and controversial career, continues to play County cricket for Hampshire but always seemed to reserve some of his best performances for games against England. Few who saw it will forget the ball which bowled Mike Gatting in 1993 – it pitched outside leg and, to the total bemusement of Mr Gatting, proceeded to clatter into the off stump. On Boxing Day 2006 Warne became the first bowler to take 700 Test wickets, when he dismissed Andrew Strauss at the Melbourne Cricket Ground, and a little while later took his 1,000th wicket in Tests and ODIs combined. He can bat a bit too, but he never quite made a Test century.

Lords and Leathers

In 1935, the country suffered from what seemed to be a veritable plague of insects. Several varieties of insect appeared in abundance, and in particular there were millions of leatherjackets in the south-east of England. They began to do serious damage to the pitch at Lord's, where unemployed men were recruited to help the ground staff to dispose of them. They collected the leatherjackets on spades, put them in bags, and burned them.

Like Father, Like Son

A great many sons have followed their fathers into first-class cricket. In 1931 G. **Gunn** of Nottinghamshire scored 183 in a match against Warwickshire. His son, G. V. Gunn, made 100 not out in the same innings.

Twenty year-old Stuart **Broad** scored the winning runs in England's victory over the West Indies in the 2007 World Cup. England won by one wicket, with one ball left. Stuart's father, Chris, played in 25 Test matches between 1984 and 1989.

Mark **Ealham**, an excellent, if somewhat stocky all-rounder who is now coming towards the end of his playing career, was born in 1969. He played for Kent before moving to Nottinghamshire, and he made eight Test match appearances, as well as featuring in a large number of ODIs. His father, Alan, born in 1944, was a middle-order batsman for Kent. He was also a very accomplished and nimble fielder.

Sunil **Gavaskar**, born in 1949, was one of India's greatest ever batsmen. He played in 125 Test matches between 1971 and 1987, and averaged more than 50 with the bat. His son Rohan, born in 1976, is less accomplished but he has featured in a number of ODIs.

Vijay and Sanjay **Manjrekar** are another Indian father and son pair. Vijay was born in 1931, and played for his country in 55 Tests. He pursued technical perfection, and very nearly achieved it. Sadly, he died at the early age of 52. Sanjay, born in 1965, featured in 37 Tests and 74 ODIs.

New Zealand's Lance **Cairns**, born in 1949, was an accomplished swing bowler. He was also a powerful hitter, once hitting six sixes in an over in a one-day international against Australia. Altogether he played in

43 Tests, taking 130 wickets, and 78 ODIs, where he took another 89. His son, Chris, born in 1970, is an all-rounder who featured in 62 Tests and 215 ODIs. Chris Cairns is widely regarded as being the second best all-rounder ever to have come out of New Zealand.

Richard **Hadlee** has to be the finest all-rounder ever to have come out of New Zealand, if not the world. His father, Walter, born in 1915, was also a first-class cricketer who played in 11 Test matches. In addition, he was an administrator and was widely respected in New Zealand cricket. Walter lived to the ripe old age of 91. Richard's brother Dayle, born in 1948, also played Test cricket.

Amongst English fathers and sons, there is Alan **Butcher**, who was born in 1954 and featured in just one Test match and one ODI, and son Mark, a left-handed batsman and right-arm bowler who has featured in 71 Tests and 255 ODIs.

Then there is Mickey **Stewart**, born in 1932, who captained Surrey from 1963 until 1972, and later became that county's cricket manager. He played in only eight Tests, but scored 385 runs. A great close catcher, it's easy to see where his son, England wicketkeeper/batsman Alec, picked up his outstanding ability.

CRICKET

Denis **Compton** of Middlesex was born in 1918. He was an incredible batsman, with a batting average of 50.06 in 78 Tests, and accomplished slow left-arm bowler. His brother Leslie was also a cricketer and, like Denis, he played football for Arsenal. Denis's grandson, Nick, who was born in Durban in 1983, now plays cricket for Middlesex.

Yorkshire and England legend Len **Hutton**'s son Richard played five Test matches for England in 1971, and also played for Yorkshire. Len's grandson, Ben, born in 1977, plays for Middlesex.

Bat and Ball

Ian Botham has achieved the feat of scoring a hundred and taking five wickets an amazing six times. Botham has also done it twice in the same match against India at Bombay in 1980. He and Jacques Kallis have also achieved the feat of scoring a hundred, a fifty and taking five wickets in the same match. Botham did it in the Ashes series against England in 1981 at Headingley while Kallis did it against the West Indies at Cape Town in 1999.

In the Teens

Surrey were all out for 14 in their first innings, in a match against Essex at Chelmsford in 1983 – Essex bowler Norbert Philip taking 6 wickets for 4 runs in 7.3 overs. Surrey did rather better in their second innings and the match, affected as it was by bad weather, ended as a draw.

For the Record: Test Matches IV

India's Sachin Tendulkar scored seven centuries before his 21st birthday. At Edgbaston in 1996, he reached a century with a six off Kent and England's Min Patel.

At the Oval in 1996, Wasim Akram took his 299th and 300th Test wickets with consecutive balls.

Derek Underwood's last Test match was Sri Lanka's first. It was played in Colombo during 1982, and Deadly Derek had match figures of 8 for 95.

The debut of Zimbabwe's first black cricketer, Henry Olonga, was postponed because it turned out that he held only a Kenyan passport.

Denis Compton was a fine batsman, who averaged more than 50 in Test cricket. However, in the 1950–51 series against Australia, he scored just 53 runs, at an average of 7.57. Still, he did pick up an FA Cup winner's medal with Arsenal in 1950.

Playing against the West Indies at Lord's in May 2007,

CRICKET

Monty Panesar became the first spinner ever to get five LBWs in a single test innings.

The record for the highest score chased by a team in the fourth innings of a Test match is 406/6 by India against the West Indies at Port of Spain in 1975–76. India needed to score 403 to win and did so.

The record for the lowest score by a team in a Test match is held by New Zealand, who scored 28 against England at Auckland in 1954–55.

The lowest fourth innings score that was successfully defended by a team in a Test match was by Australia against England in the Test match at the Oval in 1882. England needed 85 to win but they were bowled out for 77, thereby giving victory to Australia by 7 runs.

The Twenty20 Cup

Played at twenty overs apiece as the name suggests, the Twenty20 Cup is the latest form of crowd-pleasing cricket. As games can last less than three hours, other activities are provided for the spectators to make a day of it. The first competition in 2003 was won by Surrey.

The standard rules of cricket apply, but limits on fielding positions and shorter boundaries encourage positive batting. No balls win batsmen a 'free hit', while new batsmen have just 90 seconds to reach the crease or be timed out. Ties are decided by a 'bowl-off' at unguarded stumps.

Many games are played in the evening to attract those whose daytime is spent in work or school. Dismissals and boundaries are often accompanied by loud music over the PA system, enraging traditionalists but (presumably) entertaining youth.

The final, played at Edgbaston in August, is preceded on that day by the semi-finals, making this a major day out for supporters of no fewer than four counties.

More Lovable Umpires

Steve Bucknor was born in Montego Bay, Jamaica, in 1946. He was a maths teacher and sports coach, before in time becoming an international football referee and cricket umpire. He soon became a very good umpire, and he came to be regarded as honest and fair by players across the world. He umpired his first Test and his first ODI in 1989. When he stood in the West Indies in 2007, it was his fourth series of matches as a World Cup umpire. No umpire's career is entirely without its ups and downs, and Steve Bucknor has naturally at times been accused of making bad decisions. He clearly doesn't enjoy such criticism, as he once accused TV companies of deliberately trying to make umpires look bad. He is noted for long pauses before making decisions, but batsmen know that if Umpire Bucknor doesn't soon shake his head in ponderous fashion, the dreaded finger will be raised in due course.

Former Test match umpire **Darrell Hair** was born in Mudgee, New South Wales, in 1952. He is loved by Asian supporters everywhere. Or not, as the case may be. In many ways a well-respected umpire, during a Test match in Australia in December 1995, Hair no-balled Sri Lanka's Muttiah Muralitharan seven times in three overs because of his bowling action. This caused all sorts of problems and led to Hair being accused of racism by many Asians. It is certainly true that many of his more controversial decisions have involved teams from the sub-continent. In August 2006, when England met Pakistan at the Oval, Hair and fellow umpire Billy Doctrove decided that the Pakistanis had been ball-tampering. They duly awarded England five penalty runs. In protest, Pakistan refused to take the field after tea. They then decided they would continue the game, but by this time the umpires had abandoned the match and awarded it to England. The controversy rumbled on for many months and Darrell Hair was later banned from umpiring international matches.

Brent Fraser Bowden, known as Billy, was born in Auckland, New Zealand, in 1963. He developed arthritis while he was in his twenties, so he turned to umpiring. He made his ODI debut in 1995, and his Test debut in 2000. From the beginning it was clear that he had exceptional decision-making skills, but he is best known for his exaggerated signalling, for leaping about all over the place, and for raising a bent finger when a batsman is adjudged to be out.

Azhar To Do It

Ex-India captain Mohammad Azharuddin achieved the unique distinction of scoring a hundred in each of his first three Test matches in 1984–85, including his debut innings against England at Calcutta.

Cricketing Dynasties

The **Edrich** family of Norfolk must be one of the most prolific, as far as providing cricketers is concerned. And Norfolk does not even have a County Championship side. Altogether, five Edriches have played first-class cricket, four of them brothers. The best known of the four siblings was Bill Edrich, of Middlesex. A prodigious batsman and accomplished fast bowler, he played in 39 Test matches and had a batting average of 40.

Bill's brothers Eric and Geoffrey both played for Lancashire, while Brian played for Kent and Glamorgan. Cousin John was the other well-known

CRICKET

Edrich. He was the most famous of all – a brave opening batsman who made 77 Test appearances between 1963 and 1976. John's highest score was 310 not out against New Zealand at Headingley in 1965, and his Test batting average was 43.54.

In earlier days, the **Lillywhite** family from Sussex was noted for the production of cricketers – as well as for the sale of cricket gear. Fred – who became a sports outfitter – was born in Hove in 1829. He was a son of Frederick William Lillywhite (1792–1854), a very famous Sussex bowler, and the younger brother of batsman and later umpire John Lillywhite (1826–74). Fred was also a cousin of James Lillywhite (1842–1929) who captained England in first Test against Australia, in Melbourne during 1877. Lillywhites' sports shop still exists in Lower Regent Street, London.

Sussex is good at breeding cricketers. In 1930, brothers James Horace (born 1903) and Henry William **Parks** (born 1906) each scored a century for Sussex in the same innings. James Horace Parks made just a single Test appearance, but his son Jim (born 1931), a batsman and wicketkeeper, played for England in 46 Tests. Jim's son, Bobby, later played for Hampshire.

The West Indies has the distinction of providing three generations of Test match cricketers from one family. George Alfonso **Headley** was born in Panama in 1909, where his father helped build the Panama Canal. George's first language was Spanish. He was taken to Jamaica at the age of ten – his father's intention being that he should then go on to America to study to be a dentist. Instead he became the first great black batsman in the West Indies. He was in fact known in English and Australian circles as the 'Black Bradman'. West Indians were, however, rather fond of calling Bradman the 'White Headley'.

Like his father, George's son Ron (Ronald George Alfonso) Headley played for the West Indies, but he featured in just two Tests in 1973. Ron's son, Dean Warren Headley, was born in Worcestershire in 1970. He played for Kent and Middlesex, and made 15 Test appearances for England. Dean was a seam bowler, who would probably have played more games for England had he not suffered from a dodgy back.

Nanik Amarnath Bhardwaj (commonly known as Lala) **Amanarth** was born in 1911. He was the first player to score a century for India in a Test match and the first Test captain of independent India in 1947. A controversial and at times rebellious figure, Lala, a Hindu, nevertheless did what he could to encourage friendship between Hindus and Muslims during a difficult period in Indian and Pakistani history. Lala's sons, Mohinder and Surinder, both played for India too.

CRICKET

Colin **Cowdrey** (1932–2000), the son of a cricket-playing tea planter in India, was one of Kent and England's finest batsmen. He played in 114 Test matches between 1954 and 1975, and had a batting average of 44.06. His two sons, Chris and Graham, did not match their father's achievements, but both played for Kent and Chris featured in six Test matches and three ODIs.

Test Grounds of the World II

Until the tsunami struck **Galle** in December 2004, the Sri Lankan ground was viewed as one of the most beautiful venues on the Test circuit, with the Indian Ocean on either side and the 16th-century Dutch fort just outside the ground a unique landmark.

Sadly, the pavilion containing the dressing rooms and administration offices, the various VIP sections and the scoreboard that stood on the grass embankment known as 'The Hill' were lost to the waves. Such luminaries as Shane Warne and Ian Botham have both been involved in encouraging the continuation of cricket in the area and the rebuilding of the stadium.

The **Bourda** ground in Georgetown, Guyana, West Indies is one of only two Test venues in the world to sit below sea level and is accordingly protected by a moat. This location has been described as having an 'antique feel' and, affectionately by cricket writer Mike Selvey, 'slightly scruffy'. The Bourda's reputation for volatility was established in the 1970s when two disputed decisions against West Indian batsmen prompted unpleasant pitch invasions, while a Kerry Packer World Series game's abandonment caused a riot that reportedly led to players sheltering in the dressing rooms for protection.

The **Queen's Park Oval** in Port of Spain, Trinidad is the largest cricket ground in the Caribbean and reportedly the most profitable. For many a year the original pavilion, built in 1896, stood at the heart of the ground and was not replaced until 1952. The pavilion is situated at the southern end opposite the Media Centre end. On the off side three stands named after West Indian cricketing stalwarts are to be found, the trio being Learie Constantine, Jeff Stollmeyer and Dos Santos. Before being renamed, the Constantine had carried the unprepossessing soubriquet of the 'Concrete Stand', but has remained a hotbed of passionate local support.

One of the most fascinating facts about the **Recreation Ground** in Antigua involves the ground staff who, for a period, were supplied by the local prison whose warden was Malcolm Richards, the father of local hero Viv.

CRICKET

Middlesex Marvels

In 1947 Denis Compton featured in 30 first-class matches and scored a magnificent 3,816 runs at an average of 90.85. In the same year his Middlesex team-mate Bill Edrich also played in 30 matches, scoring an almost as magnificent 3,539 runs at 80.43. Those were the days.

For the Record: County Cricket II

When Lancashire scored 166–0 declared and 66–0 at Old Trafford in 1956, they became the first county side to win a match without losing a wicket.

During a game against Northamptonshire in 1967, ten different Leicestershire fielders took catches in one innings.

In 1963, nine Middlesex players arrived late for the second day's play against Kent at Tunbridge Wells. Before the missing nine arrived, Middlesex were forced to declare their innings closed and then borrow eight substitute fielders from the home side.

A tie is a comparatively rare occurrence in County cricket, but Nottinghamshire tied with Worcestershire at Trent Bridge in 1993.

Somerset were founded in 1875. No surprise there, but the founding fathers actually got things going in Sidmouth, Devon.

Tony Lock took 16 for 83 for Surrey against Kent at Blackheath in 1956.

Robin Marler of Sussex bowled three deliveries with three different balls in a match against Worcestershire, at Hove in 1955. The ground is not a large one, and Bob Broadbent had hit the first two into the middle distance – with neither being recovered.

In 1994, Warwickshire's West Indies Wonder Brian Lara became the first batsman to hit seven centuries in eight first-class innings.

In a match against Yorkshire in 1933, Worcestershire wicketkeeper Frank Ahl went on to bowl – and took four wickets.

In a match against Warwickshire in 1896, four Yorkshire players scored centuries in the same innings. This was the first time such a feat was accomplished.

Loo-ks Suspicious

Denis Compton's first County Championship match for Middlesex was against Sussex in 1936. He batted at

Number 11 and made 14 runs before umpire Bill Bestwick gave him out LBW. Bestwick admitted afterwards that the young Compton should not have been given out, and that he had only raised the finger because he, Bestwick, was desperate to spend a penny and needed to get off the field as soon as possible.

Talking Cricket IV

SIGHT SCREEN

Sight screens are placed at either end of the ground so that a batsman can pick up the flight of the ball against a plain background. The sight screens are usually white, although black ones are employed for games under floodlights, where a white ball is used. Spectators who should know better often interrupt play by wandering in front of the sight screen, totally oblivious to the chaos they are about to cause. Batsmen and umpires then proceed to shout at them until they suddenly become aware that they're causing a hold-up. Guilty spectators then usually sit down at once, spilling their beer in the process.

SLEDGING

Sledging is the practice of insulting batsmen while they are at the crease, in order to disrupt their concentration. Sometimes batsmen will also have a bit of a sledge at the bowler. It is widely accepted that sledging began in Australia, but these days everyone is at it. In some ways it is a bit like the repetitive and mindless chanting heard at football grounds – it doesn't do much good and it's very boring.

STUMPED
A batsman is stumped when the wicketkeeper breaks his wicket with the ball whilst said batsman is out of the crease. Fast bowlers hardly ever get batsmen stumped, as the wicketkeeper is forced to stand too far back. Many spin bowlers, on the other hand, rely on the agility of wicketkeepers to effect this kind of dismissal.

TIE
A tie should not be confused with a draw, as it is entirely different. A tie occurs when a match finishes with the scores even. This doesn't happen very often. A draw is the result of a match which cannot be completed due to time having run out. This happens quite a lot.

TWENTY20
The latest manifestation of one-day cricket is the Twenty20 match. This aberration, designed to attract young people to cricket matches, where they can sing, dance, spend their money, mess around and not watch any cricket, seems to be gaining in popularity. It is a limited-over game, with twenty overs per side – and everyone slogs the ball as much as possible.

CRICKET

There will no doubt be variations on Twenty20 in the future. Watch out for Ten10, Five5 and then One1. Throughout all these games, refreshments will be served at prices which would make W. G. Grace turn in his grave.

The Benson & Hedges Cup

The third major one-day competition established in England after the Sunday League and ECB Cup was held from 1972 to 2002. The first-class counties were joined by three other teams, Minor Counties (North), Minor Counties (South) and Cambridge University who alternated with Oxford. The final was played at Lord's in late June.

Scotland entered the competition in 1980 when the Minor Counties were combined to a single team. Durham joined in 1992, and Ireland in 1994 when the competition was turned into a straight knockout format.

When a ban on tobacco advertising deprived the cup of its sponsor it was replaced in 2002 by the Twenty20 Cup, first held the following year.

Well Held

Wally Hammond, the outstanding Gloucestershire and England slip fielder, held ten catches in a match (four in the first innings, six in the second) when Goucestershire played Surrey at Cheltenham on 16–17 August 1928.

Dismissed

There are ten ways in which batsmen can be dismissed in cricket:

Bowled
Caught
Handled Ball
Hit Ball Twice
Hit Wicket
Leg Before Wicket
Obstructed Field
Run Out
Stumped
Timed Out